THE
Soup Cookbook
by Dr. Duane R. Lund

More than *150*
Soup, Stew and Chili Recipes!

no stories • no pictures • no clutter . . .

. . . just 150 tried and true great recipes collected all over the
United States and in seventeen foreign countries.

Distributed by
Adventure Publications, Inc.
P.O. Box 269
Cambridge, MN 55008

ISBN 1-885061-57-9

Dedication

To my good friend, the late,
Max Ruttger III,
gracious host and chef extraordinary.

TABLE OF CONTENTS

Cauliflower and Broccoli Soups
(may use either broccoli or cauliflower)

Creamy Cauliflower / *23*
Broccoli with other Vegetables / *24*
Cauliflower - Cheese Soup / *24*
Broccoli Soup with Potatoes / *25*

Celery Soups
Cream of Celery Soup #1 / *25*
Cream of Celery Soup #2 / *26*

Cheese Soups
Cheese with Ham / *26*
Beer Cheese Soup / *27*
Cheesy Vegetable Soup / *27*
Spicy Cheese Soup / *28*
Cheesy Garden Chowder / *28*

Chicken and Turkey Soups
(using either turkey or chicken)

Chicken Gumbo / *29*
Zesty Turkey Soup / *29*
Chicken Vegetable Soup / *30*
Chicken Soup with Sweet Peppers / *31*
Left-over Turkey Soup / *31*

Consommé Recipes
Traditional Consommé / *32*
Campers' Consommé with Vegetables / *32*

Corn Soups
Spicy Corn Chowder / *33*
Chicken Corn Chowder / *33*
Corn and Potato Chowder / *34*

Fish and Seafood Soups and Chowders

New England Chowder / *34*

White Fish Chowder / *35*

Seafood Chowder / *35*

Clam Chowder / *36*

Seafood Soup / *36*

Louisiana Fish Gumbo / *37*

Florida Gumbo / *37*

Smoked Fish Soup / *38*

Hamburger Soups

Hamburger and Vegetable Soups / *38*

Cheesy Hamburger Soup / *39*

Ground Beef with Vegetable Medley / *40*

Lentil Soups

Ruttger's Lentil Soup / *40*

Green Lentil Soup / *41*

Lentils and Chickpeas / *41*

Lentils and Spinach Soups / *42*

Mushroom Soups

Quick and Creamy Mushroom Soup / *42*

Mushroom Soup with Celery and Onions #1 / *43*

Mushroom Soup with Celery and Onions #2 / *43*

Mushroom with Lentils / *44*

Onion Soups

Quick Onion Soup / *44*

Onion and Garlic Soup / *45*

Garden Onion Soup / *45*

Olive Soup

Cream of Olive Soup / *46*

Parsnip Soups

Parsnips with Rutabagas / *46*
Parsnips with Cashews / *47*

Pea Soups

Peas Soup with Ham Bone / *47*
Split Pea Soup with Potatoes / *48*
Puréed Fresh Green Pea Soup / *48*
Creamed Pea Soup using Canned Peas / *49*
Split Pea - Bean Soup / *49*

Potato Soups

Potato with Onion / *50*
Potato with Corn / *51*
Deer Camp Potato Soup / *51*
Quick and Rich Potato Soup / *52*
Potato Soup with Spinach / *52*
Baked Potato Soup / *53*
Potato with Tomato / *53*
Potato Soup with Carrots and a Hint of Orange / *54*
Potato Soup with Bacon or Ham / *54*
Sweet Potato Soup / *55*

Pumpkin and Squash Soups

Pumpkin Soup in the Shell / *56*
Squash Soup / *56*
Pumpkin Soup / *57*
Creamy Pumpkin Soup / *57*
Quick Pumpkin with Apple / *58*
Zucchini Soup / *58*

Radish Soup

Cream of Radish Soup / *59*

Spinach Soups
Spinach with Cheese / *59*
Spinach with Tortellini Soup / *60*
Spinach with Tomato / *60*

Tomato Soups
Fresh Garden Tomato / *61*
Quick Tomato Bisque / *61*
Creamy Tomato Soup / *62*
Really Creamy Tomato Soup / *62*
Tomato with Onion and Celery / *63*

Turtle Soups
Traditional Turtle Soup / *64*
Turtle Gumbo / *64*

Vegetable Soups
Vegetarian Minestrone / *65*
Minestrone with Beef / *66*
Vegetable Soup with Ham / *66*
Quick Vegetable Beef Soup / *67*
Cheesy Garden Chowder / *68*

Wild Rice Soups
Wild Rice with Chicken / *68*
Wild Rice with Mushrooms / *69*
Wild Rice with Vegetables and Beef / *70*
Wild Rice Scotch Broth with Venison / *70*
Creamy Wild Rice Soup / *71*
Washday Soup / *71*

PART II   SOUPS FROM OTHER LANDS

PART III   CHILLED SOUPS

Part I
HOT SOUPS

ARTICHOKE SOUPS
Cream of Artichoke Soup #1

Ingredients to serve 4:

1 cn. artichoke hearts (14 oz.) (cut bite-size)
2 T onion, chopped fine
1/2 t minced garlic
1 T butter or margarine or oil
4 T flour
1/2 cup white wine
1 t poultry seasoning
1/2 t thyme
2 cups milk
1 cup cream
chopped chives for garnish

Sauté the onion and garlic in the butter (or margarine or oil) 2 minutes or until onion is translucent. Place onion and garlic in a soup pot.

Add one cup of milk and stir in seasonings. Bring to a boil but reduce heat immediately to simmer; cook 5 minutes.

Stir the flour into the remaining cup of milk; add to the pot, stirring all the while. Continue to simmer. As soup begins to thicken, add artichoke hearts (including liquid from the can) and continue to cook and stir another 3 minutes or until soup is the desired consistency. Stir in wine and cream. Cook another minute or two but do not let boil. Serve piping hot.

Garnish each bowl with chopped chives.

Cream of Artichoke Soup #2

Ingredients to serve 4:

1 pkg. (9 oz.) frozen artichoke hearts
1 rib celery, chopped fine
1 carrot, sliced very thin
4 T minced onion
1 t minced garlic
3 T butter or margarine or oil
1 cup chicken broth (stock or canned will do)
3 T flour (all purpose)
1 t poultry seasoning
2 cups milk
1 cup cream
salt and pepper to taste
chopped parsley for garnish

Sauté the carrot, celery, onion and garlic in the butter or margarine or oil a few minutes or until celery and carrots are soft. Stir in the artichoke hearts and chicken broth. Place in a blender and purée until smooth.

Return to soup pot over medium heat. Stir in one cup of milk. Add the flour to the remaining cup of milk and stir until smooth. Add to the soup pot, stirring all the while. If it starts to boil, reduce heat to simmer. Soup will thicken. Stir in cream and add poultry seasoning and salt and pepper to taste. Serve piping hot but do not let boil. Stop heating at desired consistency; the longer you cook it, the thicker it will become.

Garnish each bowl with parsley (sprig or chopped).

ASPARAGUS SOUPS

Spring Garden Asparagus

Ingredients to serve 6:

4 cups chicken broth
2-1/2 cups asparagus, trimmed and cut bite-size
8 leeks, white parts only, sliced thin
1 t lemon juice
salt and pepper to taste
4 T chives, chopped, for garnish
option: 1 cup sliced mushrooms

Place all contents (except chives) in a soup pot. Bring to a boil then reduce heat to simmer. Cook 20 minutes or until asparagus is tender.

Sprinkle chives over each bowl for garnish.

Cream of Asparagus

Ingredients to serve 4:

1 pkg. frozen (or 2 cups fresh) asparagus, trimmed and cut bite-size
1 rib celery, chopped
2 T chopped onion
2 cups cream
1 cup chicken broth
2 T butter or margarine, melted or oil
salt and pepper to taste
2 T chopped chives or parsley for garnish

If asparagus is frozen, thaw and cook according to directions on the package. Drain.

If asparagus if fresh, cover with water; bring to a boil; reduce heat to simmer for 15 to 20 minutes or until asparagus is tender but not mushy. Drain. Cool to handle.

Meanwhile, sauté onion and celery in the melted butter a few minutes or until onion is translucent.

Combine all ingredients except chives. Purée in batches. Return to kettle and re-heat; do not let boil.

Garnish with chives or parsley.

Asparagus Soup with a Touch of Lemon

Ingredients to serve 6:

1 pound asparagus (fresh) trimmed and cut to half-inch pieces
1 onion, chopped
2 ribs celery, chopped
1 clove garlic, minced
1/8 pound butter or margarine (1/2 stick) or 4 T oil
2 cups water
2-1/2 cups half and half
3 T cornstarch
3 chicken bouillon cubes
2 T lemon juice
salt and pepper to taste
1/2 t nutmeg
thin twists of lemon peel for garnish

Sauté the onion, celery and garlic in the butter until onion is translucent. Meanwhile in a soup pot, cook the asparagus pieces in the water until tender (not mushy).

Dissolve the cornstarch in a little water and add to the soup pot along with the bouillon cubes. Bring to a boil, then reduce heat to simmer for 5 minutes, stirring all the while.

Stir in the lemon juice, cream and seasonings. Simmer for 15 minutes.

Cheesy Asparagus Soup

Ingredients to serve 6:

4-1/2 cups fresh or frozen asparagus, cut and drained
3-1/2 cups shredded cheese (cheddar goes well)
3 T butter or margarine or oil
3 T flour (all purpose)
6 cups milk or half and half (or three cups of each)
1 t nutmeg
1 T thyme (dried)
salt and pepper to taste
croutons or parsley for garnish

Melt butter in a soup pot and stir in flour until smooth.
Add all other ingredients. Heat thoroughly (do not boil) until cheese is melted.
Garnish with croutons or a sprig of parsley.

BARLEY SOUPS

Barley with Vegetables

Ingredients to serve 10-12:

1-1/2 cups barley (uncooked)
1/8 pound butter or margarine (1/2 stick) melted or 4 T oil
3 ribs celery, chopped
1 medium onion, peeled and chopped
4 garlic cloves, minced
1 large potato, peeled and chopped
2 carrots, chopped
1 parsnip, chopped
1 small rutabaga, chopped
2 qts. beef broth
1 t rosemary
1 t basil
2 bay leaves
1 t thyme
salt and pepper to taste

In the melted butter, sauté the onion, garlic and celery a few minutes or until the onion is translucent. Place in a soup kettle. Add all other ingredients and simmer 4 hours. Remove bay leaves before serving.

Barley with Beef and Vegetables

Ingredients to serve 6:

1-1/2 pounds beef stew meat, cut bite-size
1 cup chopped cabbage
1 qt. water
1 medium onion, peeled and chopped
1 cn. tomatoes, Italian style, chopped (save liquid)
2/3 cup pearl barley
1 medium potato, peeled and chopped
1/8 pound butter or margarine (1/2 stick) melted or 4 T oil
1 carrot, sliced thin
2 ribs celery, chopped
3 T catsup (for seasoning)

Sauté the onion, celery and garlic a few minutes until onion is translucent. Place in a large soup pot. Add water, beef, tomatoes and catsup. Bring to a boil, then reduce heat and simmer 1-1/2 to 2 hours or until meat is tender.

At this point you may need to add more water. Add carrots, potatoes and barley and continue to simmer for 20 minutes. Add cabbage and let simmer another 15-20 minutes our until everything is tender.

BEAN SOUPS

Southern Black Bean Soup

Ingredients to serve 6:

2-1/2 cups dried black beans
1 large smoked ham hock (discard fat and tough skin)
1 large onion, peeled and sliced; break into rings
4 cups chicken broth
2 cups water
1 t cumin
1/2 t tarragon
3 T chives, chopped, for garnish

In a soup pot, simmer all ingredients (except chives) for 1 hour. Remove ham hock and let cool until it can be handled and meat pieces cut from bone. Let soup continue to simmer. Return ham pieces (diced) to kettle and continue cooking until beans are tender.

Garnish with chopped chives (or croutons).

Crock Pot Black Bean Soup

Ingredients to serve 8:

4 cups cooked black beans
1 cup chopped onion
1/2 cup chopped green (bell) pepper
1 4 oz. cn. chopped chilies
3 cups chicken broth
1/2 cup red cooking wine
2 t minced garlic
1 t cumin
1 t tarragon

Combine all ingredients in a crock pot and cook 3 hours on high and 3 hours on low. Soup should be quite thick.
Option: Let soup cool; purée in batches and re-heat.

Spicy White Bean Soup in a Crock Pot

Ingredients to serve 8:

1 medium potato, diced
1 carrot, chopped
2 ribs celery, chopped
1 medium onion, peeled and chopped
1 parsnip, chopped
1 4 oz. cn. chopped green chilies
1-1/2 pounds dry white beans
1 pound ham, cut bite-size
6 cups water
2 bay leaves
8 drops Tabasco

Place all ingredients in a crock pot; cook 3 hours on high setting and three hours on low setting or until vegetables are tender. Remove bay leaves before serving.

Smorgasbord Bean and Pea Soup

Ingredients to serve 6:

1/8 pound butter or margarine (1/2 stick) melted or 4 T oil
1 small onion, peeled and chopped
2 carrots, sliced thin
2 ribs celery, chopped

2 cloves garlic, minced
1/4 cup of each of the following (all dry):
> yellow split peas
>
> green split peas
>
> Great Northern beans
>
> black beans
>
> kidney beans
>
> navy beans
>
> garbanzo chickpeas
>
> lentils

2 pork hocks (2 small or 1 large)
6 cups water plus enough water to cover beans and peas
1 cn. Italian style tomatoes
3 T catsup
1 t thyme
1 t rosemary
1/2 t Tabasco sauce (more if you like it more spicy)

Sauté the onion, garlic and celery a few minutes or until onion is translucent. Place the beans and peas in a soup pot and cover with water. Bring to a boil, then reduce heat to simmer for 1 hour. Drain. Place all ingredients in the soup pot with the 6 cups of water (Do not add tomatoes at this time). Bring to a boil, then reduce heat to simmer for 1 hour. Remove pork hocks and let cool while ingredients simmer another hour. Cut meat from hocks and dice. Return ham to pot along with tomatoes. Increase heat until bubbly. Serve hot.

Senate Bean Soup

The U.S. Senate restaurant is famous for its bean soup. It has been on the menu longer than anyone can remember. Originally, the recipe was a guarded secret. As the story goes, Minnesota's Senator Knute Nelson went to the restaurant one day anticipating a bowl of his favorite soup. To his disappointment they did not serve it that day. He returned to the Senate Floor and introduced a bill mandating that the soup be served every day and that the recipe be printed on the menu! Here it is, just as printed on the menu:

The Famous Senate Restaurant Bean Soup Recipe

Take two pounds of small Navy Pea Beans, wash, and run through hot water until Beans are white again. Put on the fire with four quarts of hot water. Then take one and one-half pounds of Smoked Ham Hocks, boil slowly approximately three hours in covered pot. Braise one onion chopped in a little butter, and, when light brown, put in Bean Soup. Season with salt and pepper, then serve. Do not add salt until ready to serve. *(Eight persons.)*

CABBAGE SOUPS

Cabbage with Pork

Ingredients to serve 6-8:

1 medium head cabbage - diced bite-size (about 2 pounds)
1 pound cooked pork roast, diced bite-size (if not cooked, brown pieces first)
3 medium potatoes, diced
3 carrots, scraped and diced (thick slices)
6 cups chicken broth (may use water)
12 allspice (whole)
10 peppercorns
1 bay leaf
salt to taste
4 T parsley, flakes or chopped, for garnish

Place all ingredients except parsley in boiling water. Reduce heat to simmer until meat is tender (about 1 hour if meat is tender to start with).
Remove bay leaf before serving.
Garnish with parsley.

Cabbage with other vegetables

Ingredients to serve 8:

1 medium head cabbage, shredded
1/8 pound butter or margarine (1/2 stick) melted or 4 T oil
3 medium onions, peeled, sliced and broken into rings
3 cups beef broth
3 cups water
3 carrots, sliced thin
2 potatoes, peeled and diced
3 ribs celery, chopped
3 tomatoes, diced
1 t pepper
salt to taste
sour cream to top each bowl of soup

Sauté onions, carrots and celery. Transfer to soup pot. Add all other ingredients except cabbage, tomatoes and sour cream. Bring to a boil then reduce heat to simmer; cook for 20 minutes. Add cabbage and continue to simmer another 10 minutes. Add tomatoes and continue to cook 10 minutes or until all vegetables are tender.
Serve with a dollop of sour cream on the surface of each bowl.

Cabbage Soup with Chicken

Ingredients to serve 8:

1 small chicken (stewing chicken will do)
1 head cabbage (small to medium) shredded
2 qts. water
1 large onion, sliced and broken into rings
3 T flour
2 t salt
10 whole peppercorns
3 bay leaves
chopped parsley for garnish

In a large soup pot, cover the whole chicken with the water and add the cabbage, onion, salt, peppercorns and bay leaves. Bring to a boil, then reduce to simmer and cook, covered, until chicken meat will easily come off the bones (about 1 hour). Remove the chicken, cool and remove meat from bones. Cut bite-size. Return meat to the pot, bring to a boil and reduce to simmer. Stir the flour into a little water and then stir into the soup. Cook another 10 or 15 minutes or until the soup thickens slightly. Remove bay leaves before serving.
Garnish with the chopped parsley.

Cabbage with Polish Sausage

Ingredients to serve 6-8:

1 medium cabbage, shredded
1/8 pound butter or margarine (1/2 stick) melted or 4 T oil
1 onion, peeled and chopped
3 ribs celery, chopped
3 carrots, scraped and sliced
6 cups chicken broth
4 Polish sausages, cooked and sliced (half-inch chunks)
1/3 cup flour
salt and pepper to taste
parsley springs for garnish

Sauté the onion and celery in the melted butter a couple of minutes or until onion is translucent. Stir in the flour until smooth.
Add all other ingredients; bring to a boil; reduce heat to simmer; cook about 15 minutes or until thoroughly heated and carrots are soft.
Garnish with parsley.

CARROT SOUPS

Carrot with Nuts

Ingredients to serve 4:

8 medium carrots, scraped and chopped
1/8 pound butter or margarine (1/2 stick) melted or 4 T oil
2 medium onions, peeled and chopped
1 t cumin
1/2 t pepper
2 cups chicken broth
2 cups water
1/2 cup slivered almonds*, chopped
parsley for garnish

Sauté the onions and carrots in the melted butter for 3 or 4 minutes or until the onions are translucent.

Meanwhile, put the nuts under the broiler for a few minutes until they are crisp. Watch closely; do not let burn.

Add chicken broth and water to carrots and onions and bring to a boil; reduce heat; let simmer 20 minutes or until carrots are soft. Let cool.

Mix together all ingredients and then purée in batches. Re-heat and serve hot. Garnish with parsley.

* May substitute walnuts or cashews.

Spicy Carrot Soup

Ingredients to serve 6:

1/8 pound butter or margarine (1/2 stick) melted or 4 T cooking oil
10 medium carrots, scraped and sliced thin
2 large onions, peeled and sliced and broken into rings
3 cups chicken broth
2 cups half and half
1/2 t nutmeg
1/2 t basil
1 bay leaf
1/4 t Tabasco (or to taste)
chives, chopped, for garnish

In the melted butter, sauté the carrots and onion 3 or 4 minutes, stirring and tossing so that onions do not burn. Add all other ingredients. Bring to a boil but do not let boil - reduce heat at first indication it is about to boil. Simmer 20 minutes or until carrots are soft.

Garnish with chopped chives.

Carrot Soup with Apple

Ingredients to serve 6:

8 carrots, sliced thin
2 hard apples, peeled, cored and chopped
1 onion, peeled and chopped
1 clove garlic, minced
2 ribs celery, chopped
5 cups chicken broth
1/8 pound butter (1/2 stick)
2 bay leaves
1/8 t black pepper
parsley, in sprigs or chopped for garnish

Sauté the carrots, apples, celery, onion and garlic in the butter (about 3 minutes or until the onion is translucent). Transfer to a soup kettle.

Add all other ingredients and bring to a boil. Reduce heat to simmer and cook 30 minutes or until carrots are tender. Let cool.

Remove bay leaves. Purée in batches. Return to kettle and cook until piping hot.

Garnish with parsley.

CAULIFLOWER AND BROCCOLI SOUPS

In each of the following recipes you may substitute broccoli for cauliflower and visa versa.

Creamy Cauliflower

Ingredients to serve 6-8:

1-1/2 pounds trimmed cauliflower, rinsed and diced
3 cups chicken broth
2 cups water plus enough water to cover cauliflower to start
1 cup cream
1 t curry powder (less if you don't like spicy food)
springs of parsley to garnish

Cover diced cauliflower with water. Bring to a boil; remove from heat and let stand 2 minutes. Drain and rinse with cold water.

Return cauliflower to kettle; add chicken broth, 3 cups water and curry powder. Bring to a boil, then reduce heat to simmer and cook for 15 minutes. Let cool enough to handle.

Purée in batches. Return to kettle. Stir in cream. Re-heat, thoroughly, but do not let boil.

Garnish with sprigs of parsley.

Broccoli with other Vegetables

Ingredients to serve 6:

1/8 pound butter or margarine (1/2 stick) melted or 4 T oil
2 onions, peeled and chopped
3 cloves garlic, minced
2 ribs celery, chopped
3 cups trimmed broccoli, cut bite-size
3 tomatoes, diced
3 carrots, scraped and sliced thin
1 potato, peeled and diced
1/2 t basil
1/2 t oregano
1/2 t ginger
enough water to cover broccoli to start
chives, chopped for garnish

Sauté onions, celery and garlic in melted butter.
Cover broccoli with water; bring to a boil; set aside (off heat) for 2 minutes. Drain and rinse with cold water.
Place all ingredients, except tomatoes, in a soup pot. Bring to a boil, then reduce heat to simmer and cook 20 minutes. Add tomatoes and cook another 5 minutes. Let cool (enough to handle).
Using a slotted spoon, set aside 2 cups of vegetables.
Purée rest of soup in batches.
Return all ingredients to the soup kettle and re-heat until hot throughout.
Garnish with chives.

Cauliflower - Cheese Soup

Ingredients to serve 6-8:

1 pkg. frozen cauliflower
3 cups chicken broth
3 cups milk
1 small onion, chopped
1 T butter, margarine or oil
1/2 pound American cheese, grated or chopped
6 oz. egg noodles

If there are large pieces of cauliflower, cut or break them bite-size.
Sauté the onion in butter until translucent. Place in cooking pot and add broth. Bring to a boil, then add noodles. Cook five minutes or until

tender. Reduce heat to a slow boil; add cauliflower. Cook 5 minutes. Add milk and cheese and reduce heat to simmer. Cook until cheese is melted.

You may wish to reserve a little shredded cheese for garnish on each bowl.

Broccoli Soup with Potatoes

Ingredients to serve 6:

1 onion, chopped
2 clove garlic, minced
1 rib celery, chopped
1/8 pound butter or margarine or 4 T oil
2 carrots, sliced thin
2 cups broccoli, cut bite-size
2 cups diced potatoes
4 cups chicken stock (page 105)
salt and pepper to taste
1/2 t curry powder
chopped chives for garnish

Sauté the onion, garlic, carrots and celery in the butter until onion is translucent. (do not let burn) Place in a soup pot.

Add all other ingredients and bring to a boil. Reduce heat and simmer until carrots and potatoes are tender.

Garnish each bowl with chopped chives.

CELERY SOUPS

Cream of Celery #1

Ingredients to serve 6:

3 cups chopped celery (fairly coarse)
2 medium onions, peeled and chopped
1 carrot, scraped and chopped
2 cups water
2 cups cream
1/2 t thyme
1/2 t basil
salt and pepper to taste
celery leaves, chopped, for garnish

Cover celery, onions and carrots with water. Add seasonings. Bring to a boil; reduce heat; let simmer 20 minutes or until celery and carrots are tender.

Stir in cream and continue heating until hot throughout. Do not boil. Garnish with chopped celery leaves.

(This soup may be puréed, in which case add the cream after using the blender. It then may be served hot or chilled.)

Cream of Celery #2

Use the same recipe as above but substitute:

1 medium diced potato for the carrot
1 t minced garlic for the thyme and basil

Add 1/2 cup white wine at the end when you add the cream.

CHEESE SOUPS

Cheese with Ham

Ingredients to serve 6:

2 medium onions, peeled and chopped
3 ribs celery, chopped
1/8 pound butter or margarine (1/2 stick) or 4 T oil
3 medium carrots, scraped and sliced thin
2 garlic cloves, minced
1-1/2 cups cooked ham, diced
3/4 pound cheese of your choosing. American or Cheddar work well
3 cups chicken broth
2 cups milk (for richer soup, use half and half)
2 T flour
1/8 t pepper (use a little less with cheddar cheese)
1/2 t mustard (ground)
popcorn for garnish

Sauté onion, celery and garlic a few minutes or until onion is translucent, transfer to a soup kettle.

Add all ingredients except cheese and flour. Bring to a boil, reduce to simmer; cook 20 minutes or until carrots are tender.

Stir in flour. Continue to cook until soup starts to thicken (no more than 3 minutes).

Grate or cut cheese into small cubes. Add to the soup and continue to heat until the cheese melts.

Garnish with popcorn.

Beer Cheese Soup*

Ingredients to serve 4:

1/4 pound (1 stick) butter or margarine or 8 T oil
1/2 t seasoned salt
1/4 t celery salt
1 t Worcestershire sauce
1/2 cup diced onion
1/4 cup diced celery
1/2 cup flour
2 cns. condensed chicken broth
1 cn. (12 oz.) beer
2 cups shredded cheddar cheese
popcorn for garnish (optional)

Melt butter in a large saucepan; add seasonings; onions and celery. Cook over medium heat until vegetables are softened. Add flour, whisking to blend. Cook until bubbly; reduce heat to low and add remaining ingredients, whisking until cheese melts.
Garnish with popcorn (optional).

*Courtesy Max Ruttger III, Gull Lake, Minnesota

Cheesy Vegetable Soup

Ingredients to serve 4:

1/8 pound butter or margarine (1/2 stick) or 4 T oil
1 onion, peeled and chopped
2 medium carrots. scraped and chopped
2 celery ribs, chopped
2 medium potatoes, peeled and diced
1 green bell pepper seeded and chopped
2 cups chicken broth
4 T flour
1-1/2 cups water
4 oz. cheddar cheese, grated or diced small
1/2 t cumin
1/2 t thyme
1 t pepper
chopped celery leaves for garnish

Sauté onions, celery, pepper and carrots 2 or 3 minutes until onion is translucent. Move to a soup pot. Sprinkle in flour and continue to heat and stir another 2 or 3 minutes.

Add all other ingredients except the cheese. Bring to a boil, then reduce heat to simmer and cook another 15 minutes or until the potatoes and carrots are soft.

Stir in the cheese until it is all melted.

Garnish with celery leaves.

Spicy Cheese Soup

Ingredients to serve 4:

8 oz. cheddar cheese, shredded or cut into very small pieces
1 onion, peeled and chopped fine
1/8 pound butter or margarine (1/2 stick) or 4 T oil
2 ribs celery, chopped fine
2 T flour
1 clove garlic, minced
6 drops Tabasco (or to taste)
2 cns. chicken broth
2 cups half and half
garnish with popcorn (optional)

Sauté onion, celery and garlic in butter 2 or 3 minutes. Sprinkle in flour and continue to stir and cook 2 minutes. Transfer to pot.

Add all remaining ingredients except cheese. Heat (but do not boil) for 10 minutes. Add cheese and stir until it is all melted.

Popcorn is the traditional garnishment.

Cheesy Garden Chowder

Ingredients to serve 8:

1 medium onion, chopped
2 ribs celery, chopped
1 medium zucchini, sliced thin
3 T butter or margarine or oil
6 medium tomatoes, diced (may substitute canned)
2 cups fresh corn (may substitute frozen or whole kernel canned)
1 cup fresh peas (may substitute frozen)
2 cups milk
2 cups chicken broth or stock (page 105)
1 bay leaf
1 t basil
2 cups shredded cheddar cheese
salt and pepper to taste
chopped chives or parsley for garnish

Sauté the onion, celery and zucchini a few minutes or until the squash is soft. Place in a soup pot.

Add all ingredients except the milk, tomatoes and cheese.

Bring to a boil, then reduce heat and cook until the corn is tender.

Add milk, tomatoes and cheese and continue to cook (but not boil) until the cheese is melted. Stir occasionally.

Remove bay leaf before serving.

Garnish with chives or parsley.

CHICKEN AND TURKEY SOUPS*

Chicken Gumbo

Ingredients to serve 8:

white breast meat from a large chicken, cut up bite-size
1/2 cup flour
1/4 pound butter or margarine, melted or 8 T oil
1 large onion, peeled, sliced and broken into rings
3 ribs celery, chopped
3 cloves garlic, minced
1 green pepper, seeded and chopped
6 cups chicken broth
2 cns. tomato sauce
3 smoked, cooked Polish sausages, sliced (1/2 inch thick)
1/2 pound pre-cooked ham, cut bite-size
1/2 pound shrimp, uncooked, fresh or frozen, tails removed
1 lg. cn. black beans
1 cup okra, chopped
salt and pepper to taste
3 cups cooked rice

Sauté chicken pieces (dredged in the flour) in the melted butter. Onion, celery and garlic may be cooked at the same time. Brown the chicken pieces on all sides - no red showing. Place in a large soup pot.

Add all other ingredients except rice, okra and shrimp. Bring to a boil and then reduce heat to simmer for 30 minutes. Add Okra and shrimp and continue cooking another 10 minutes. Serve over rice placed in each bowl.

Zesty Turkey Soup

Ingredients to serve 6:

1 pound left-over turkey, cut bite-size (either dark or light meat)
4 cups chicken broth
2 cns. whole kernel corn

Turkey may be exchanged for chicken and visa versa

1 4 oz. cn. Jalapeno peppers (cut up-use kitchen gloves)
1 small green pepper, seeded and chopped
1 2 oz. jar pimentos
1 cup salsa (mild, medium or hot - your choice)
1 t chili powder
1 t cumin
2 cups tortilla chips, broken
4 oz. cheese (your choice; Monterey Jack works well) shredded - for garnish

In a large soup kettle, combine all ingredients except the chips and corn. Bring to a boil and then reduce to simmer for 10 minutes.
Add corn and continue to cook another 8 minutes.
Place equal amounts of tortilla chips in each bowl. Add soup.
Garnish each bowl with shredded cheese.

Chicken Vegetable Soup

Ingredients to serve 8:

1 pound left-over chicken, cut bite-size
1/8 pound butter or margarine (1/2 stick) or 4 T oil
3 ribs celery, chopped
3 medium carrots, scraped and sliced thin
3 parsnips, scraped and diced
2 large onions, peeled and chopped
2 large potatoes, peeled and diced
1/2 pound fresh mushrooms (or 1/4 pound canned) sliced
1 cn. whole kernel corn
1/2 cup barley, rinsed and soaked 1 hour
1/2 cup dried peas, rinsed and soaked 1 hour
4 cups chicken broth
1 T poultry seasoning
seasoned croutons for garnish (or sprigs of dill)

Sauté the onion and celery in butter 2 or 3 minutes until onion is translucent. Place in a soup pot.
Add all other ingredients except corn. Bring to a boil, then reduce heat to simmer for 30 minutes. Add corn and continue to simmer 10 minutes or until all vegetables are tender.
Garnish with croutons or sprigs of dill.

Chicken Soup with Sweet Peppers

Ingredients to serve 6:

1 large onion, chopped
3 cloves garlic, minced
4 ripe tomatoes, diced (may substitute canned)
1 large green bell pepper, seeded and cut into narrow slices
1 large red bell pepper, seeded and cut into narrow slices
4 cups chicken stock (page 105) or broth
1 pound skinned, boneless chicken breast, diced bite-size
1 cn. (#2 size) chick-peas
4 T cooking oil or olive oil
3 T chopped parsley or parsley flakes
1/2 t poultry seasoning
1/4 t pepper and salt to taste
parsley sprigs for garnish

Slice the peppers into thin strips and then cut the strips into approximately 1 inch segments. Cook the pepper strips in the oil and over low heat until tender, about 15 minutes. Remove the pepper strips and cook the onion and garlic a few minutes or until onion is translucent. Place pepper strips, onion and garlic in a soup pot and add all other ingredients except the tomatoes and chick peas. Bring to a boil, then reduce heat and cook about 15 minutes, stirring occasionally. When chicken is cooked through, add tomatoes and chick peas and cook another 5 minutes.

Serve hot and garnish each bowl with a sprig of parsley.

note: If red bell peppers are not available, pimentos may be substituted.

Left-over Turkey Soup*

Ingredients to serve 4-5:

Bones (carcass) of a 12-14 pound turkey
7 cups water
3 ribs celery, chopped
2 carrots, diced
1 small onion, chopped
1/2 cup uncooked rice
1 T salt
2 cups milk
2 sprigs parsley, chopped for garnish

Crack the turkey bones, add water, celery, carrots and onion. Cover, let simmer 1-1/2 hours. Remove the bones. Cool to handle. Blend soup in batches and return to the kettle.

Return broth to boiling. Add rice and salt. Simmer 30 minutes or until the rice is done.

Add milk. Re-heat but do not boil.

Garnish with parsley.

*Courtesy Barbara Olson, Anchorage, Alaska

Traditional Consommé

Ingredients to serve 6:

8 cups beef (or veal) stock (page 106)
1 cup chopped beef or veal
3 T chopped onion
1 carrot, scraped and sliced thin
2 ribs celery, chopped
1 T chopped parsley
3 eggs, whites only
1/2 t salt
6 peppercorns
1/2 cup white wine
chives or parsley for garnish

Beat egg whites into a froth.

Combine all ingredients except the wine in a soup pot. Bring to a boil, then reduce heat to simmer for 30 minutes. Eggs will float to the top. Let cool to handle. Pour through a fine sieve and discard solids. Return liquid to pot and re-heat. Add wine a minute or two before removing from heat. If you wish to remove alcoholic content, add wine immediately after straining.

Garnish with chives or parsley.

May be served hot or chilled.

Campers' Consommé with Vegetables

Ingredients to serve 6-8:

1 cup consommé (or can)
2 envelopes dry vegetable soup mix

Add water as per directions on the envelope but substitute 1 cup or can of consommé for part of the water called for.

CORN SOUPS

Spicy Corn Chowder

Ingredients to serve 6:

3 cups whole kernel corn (from the can or frozen or cut fresh off the cob)
1-1/2 cups chicken broth
1 cup cream
3 Jalapeno peppers, seeded and chopped (use kitchen gloves)
(or 1-4 oz. cn. chopped Jalapeno peppers)
1 sm. jar (2 oz.) pimentos, chopped

Purée half of the corn, peppers and broth in a blender.
Combine all ingredients in a soup pot. Heat thoroughly but do not boil.

Chicken Corn Chowder

Ingredients to serve 6-8:

2 chicken breast halves, skinned and cut bite-size
1 cn. whole kernel corn
1 cn. cream style corn
1 4 oz. cn. chopped Jalapeno peppers
1/4 pound butter or margarine (1 stick) melted or 8 T oil
1 small onion, peeled and chopped
2 cloves garlic, minced
2 ribs celery, chopped
2 cups chicken broth
1/2 pound Monterey Jack cheese, grated
2 cups cream
1 t cumin
1 t oregano
2 tomatoes, diced
flour to brown chicken
croutons for garnish

Roll the chicken pieces in flour. Sauté the chicken, onion, celery and garlic until chicken is brown (no pink showing).
Combine all ingredients, except tomatoes, in a soup pot. Heat (do not let boil) until cheese melts. Add tomatoes. Let simmer another 5 minutes.
Garnish with croutons.

Corn and Potato Chowder

Ingredients to serve 6:

1 onion, chopped
2 strips bacon, cut crossways into narrow strips
1 rib celery, chopped
2 large potatoes, peeled and diced
2 cns. whole kernel corn (Mexican if available)
1 cn. chicken broth
1 cn. water
2 cups milk
2 T flour
salt and pepper to taste
parsley flakes (or chopped fresh) for garnish

Place the chopped bacon in the bottom of a soup pot over medium heat. As soon as grease appears, add chopped onion and celery. When bacon is crisp, add chicken broth, potatoes and water. Bring to a boil, then reduce heat to simmer for 20 minutes or until potatoes are soft. Stir the flour into about a half cup of milk, then add this mixture plus the rest of the milk to the pot. Continue to heat (do not boil) for about 5 minutes or until piping hot.
Season to taste.
Garnish with parsley.

FISH AND SEAFOOD SOUPS AND CHOWDERS
New England Chowder

Ingredients to serve 8-10:

2 pounds skinned fish fillets, deboned and cut into chunks
3 onions, sliced and broken into rings
4 large potatoes, peeled and cut into bite-size pieces
3 cups water
5 T salt
10 peppercorns
2 carrots, chunked
1 quart milk
1 cup cream

Bring the water to boiling. Add all ingredients except the fish, milk and cream. Bring to a boil and continue boiling until the potatoes and carrots are done. Stir in the milk and cream, add fish, bring to a boil, reduce heat and let simmer, covered, 20 minutes.

White Fish Chowder

Ingredients to serve 4:

1/2 cup chopped onion
1/4 cup chopped green pepper
2 T butter, margarine or oil
1 10-3/4 oz. cn. condensed tomato soup
1 14-1/2 oz. cn. evaporated milk
1 chicken bouillon cube, crushed
Dash garlic salt
1 pound fresh fish poached and flaked (2 cups)

Poach fish a few minutes (about 5) in boiling water until opaque and you can flake with a fork.

In a 3 quart saucepan cook onion and green pepper in butter until tender but not brown. Add soup, evaporated milk, bouillon cube and garlic powder. Stir in the cooked fish and heat through.

Seafood Chowder with Celery

Ingredients to serve 6:

1 cn. cream of celery soup
2 cups fish stock (see page 105)
2 cups milk
1/2 cup white wine
1/2 pound shrimp, tails removed (if large, cut bite-size)
1/2 pound lobster tail - cut bite-size (scallops may be substituted)
1 onion, chopped
1 clove garlic, minced
2 ribs celery, chopped
1/8 pound butter or margarine (1/2 stick)
salt and pepper to taste
celery leaves (whole or chopped) for garnish

Sauté the onion, celery and garlic in the butter until onion is translucent. Place in a soup pot. Add all other ingredients and bring to a boil, then reduce heat immediately and simmer 4 minutes or until seafood is opaque.

Garnish with celery leaves.

Clam Chowder

Ingredients to serve 4-5:

4 slices bacon, cut into small pieces
1 cn. clams (about 1 pint)
3 medium potatoes, diced
1 carrot, scraped and cut into thin slices
3 cups milk
1 medium onion, peeled and chopped
1/2 t basil, ground
salt and pepper to taste
oyster crackers (float on top of each bowl)

Fry bacon bits until not quite crisp. Remove bacon and save.
Sauté the chopped onion in the bacon grease until translucent.
Remove onion pieces and discard grease.
Meanwhile, boil the potatoes and carrot until soft. Remove and discard water.
In a soup pot, combine all ingredients except salt and pepper. As soon as the soup begins to boil, reduce heat to simmer. After about 20 minutes add salt and pepper to taste. Serve piping hot with oyster crackers.

Seafood Soup

Ingredients to serve 8:

2 pounds mussels or scallops or boneless fish or combinations thereof
1 lg. cn. (32 oz.) plum tomatoes, chopped (save juice)
1 large onion, broken into rings
3 T minced garlic
4 cups water
2 cups white wine
3 T chopped oregano
1/2 t Tabasco or other hot sauce
2 T olive oil
1 cup parsley, fresh, chopped
garlic toast, broken, for garnish

If you use mussels, clean, de-beard and cook in boiling water until they open.
Sauté the onion rings in the oil until translucent; do not burn.
Combine the following in a large soup kettle: water, wine, seafood, tomatoes, tomato liquid from the can, garlic, oregano and Tabasco.
Bring to a boil and then reduce heat and simmer 15 minutes or until the seafood is done.
Serve with garlic toast for garnish.

Louisiana Fish Gumbo

Ingredients to serve 6:

1/4 cup butter
1/2 cup chopped onion
1 medium-sized green pepper, chopped
1/2 cup chopped celery
1 28 oz. cn. of tomatoes
1 15-1/2 oz. cn. okra
1 cup water
1/4 t dried thyme leaves
1 t salt
1 lb. fish fillets, deboned and cut into bite-size pieces
3 cups cooked rice

Melt butter in a large saucepan over moderately low heat. Add onion, green pepper and celery. Cook until tender (about 3 or 4 minutes). Add tomatoes, okra, water, thyme and salt and simmer for 15 minutes, stirring occasionally. Add fish and cook 10 minutes or until fish is easily flaked. Spoon 1/2 cup hot rice into each soup bowl before filling with the fish mixture.

Florida Gumbo

Ingredients to serve 6:

1 pound (or more if you like) of white-meated fish, bite-size
1 rib celery, chopped
1 clove garlic, minced
1 onion, cut into rings
2 carrots, scraped and sliced
1 parsnip, scraped and sliced
1/4 pound butter or margarine (1 stick) or 8 T oil
2/3 cup of rice (uncooked)
1 cn. tomatoes, Italian style
1 qt. fish stock (see page 105)
2 bay leaves
2 T catsup
3 T chopped parsley for garnish

Sauté the vegetables, a few minutes until onion is translucent.
Place in a soup pot with the fish stock, catsup, bay leaves, rice and tomatoes; bring to a boil and then reduce heat to simmer. Cook 20 minutes or until vegetables begin to soften.
Add the fish and continue to simmer another 15 minutes.
Remove bay leaves.
Garnish with chopped parsley.

Smoked Fish Soup

Use either saltwater or freshwater fish.

Ingredients to serve 6:

2 pounds smoked fish (remove bones)
4 potatoes, peeled and cut into bite-size chunks
2 medium onions, peeled and chopped
salt to taste (other seasonings may be added, such as white pepper, thyme, dill or your favorite)
2 T parsley, chopped
4 T butter, margarine or oil
3 cups cream
parsley, chopped, for garnish

Cover the potato chunks with water and boil until done. Meanwhile, sauté the onion in the butter. Using the pan in which you sautéed the onion, add the potatoes, cream and seasonings. Simmer (do not boil) until all ingredients are hot. Serve in shallow bowls over pieces of smoked fish and garnish with the chopped parsley.

HAMBURGER SOUPS

Hamburger and Vegetable Soup

Ingredients to serve 10:

1/8 pound butter or margarine (1/2 stick) melted, or 4 T oil
1 medium onion, chopped fine
2 ribs celery, chopped fine
2 cloves garlic, minced
1-1/2 pounds ground beef
1/2 cup cracker or bread crumbs
2 t minced parsley
1 t oregano
1 t chili powder
2 potatoes, peeled and diced
3 carrots, sliced thin
2 parsnips, scraped and chopped
1 small rutabaga, diced
2 cns. tomatoes, Italian style
6 cups beef broth
1 t thyme
1 t cumin
garnish with parsley sprigs

Sauté the onion, celery and garlic in the melted butter until onion is translucent (2 or 3 minutes).

With moistened hands, thoroughly mix the hamburger, onion, celery, garlic, crumbs, parsley, oregano and chili powder. Mold into small meatballs no more than 1 inch in diameter.

Brown the meatballs in the same pan used to sauté first ingredients; add more butter if necessary. Brown all sides - about 6 to 7 minutes.

Place all ingredients (except parsley reserved for garnish) in a crockpot and cook on high for 2 hours and on low for another 2 hours or until all vegetables are soft.

Garnish bowls of soup with parsley sprigs.

Cheesy Hamburger Soup

Ingredients to serve 8:

1/4 pound butter or margarine, melted (1 stick) or 8 T oil

1 onion, peeled and chopped

2 ribs celery, chopped

3 cloves garlic, minced

1 pound hamburger

4 cups beef broth

3 medium potatoes, peeled and diced

4 carrots, scraped and sliced thin

2 cns. tomatoes, Italian style

8 oz. grated cheese of your choice (cheddar will do just fine)

2 cups cream

1 t oregano

1 t thyme

1 t basil

1/2 t salt

1/2 t pepper

seasoned croutons for garnish

In a soup kettle, sauté the onion, celery, crumbled hamburger and garlic in the melted butter until the hamburger is brown.

Add all other ingredients except the cheese, croutons and cream. Bring to a boil, then reduce heat to simmer. Cook 20 minutes or until all vegetables are soft.

Stir in cream and cheese and continue to cook (but do not boil) another 10 minutes (until the cheese has melted).

Serve with croutons as garnish.

Ground Beef with Vegetable Medley*

Ingredients to serve 4:

1/2 pound lean ground beef
3/4 cup chopped onion
3/4 cup chopped celery
3/4 cup diced potatoes
1 cn. tomatoes (do not drain) 16 oz.
1/2 Jalapeno pepper, seeded (use kitchen gloves)
2 carrots, sliced thin
1/2 bay leaf, crumbled
1/8 T diced sweet basil
1/2 T chives, chopped
1/8 T garlic powder
1/8 T thyme (dried)
1 T salt
1/4 T pepper
2 cups hot water
2 T butter or margarine or oil

Brown beef, onion and celery in the butter (until onion is translucent). Place in a soup pot (drain first).
Add all other ingredients. Bring to a boil, then reduce heat to simmer for 30 minutes or until vegetables are tender.
*Courtesy Karen Schindler, Phoenix

LENTIL SOUPS

Ruttger's Lentil Soup*

Ingredients to serve 10:

2 cups lentil beans, rinsed
2 t salt
4 cups water

Place in a covered saucepan, simmer over low heat until tender (1-1/2 hours). Water will be mostly absorbed by the beans.

2 T butter or margarine or oil
2 t seasoned salt
2 carrots, minced
2 ribs celery, minced
2 medium potatoes, peeled and diced
1 medium onion, peeled and diced

Melt butter over medium heat. Add salt. Add vegetables and sauté, tossing and stirring occasionally until softened. Add 8 cups water (if desired, 1 cup of the liquid can be dry white wine or sherry). Add lentils, simmer 1 hour, stirring occasionally.

*Courtesy Max Ruttger III, Gull Lake, Mn

Green Lentil Soup

Ingredients to serve 8:

1-1/2 cups green lentils, rinsed
1/8 pound butter or margarine (1/2 stick)
1 onion (large), peeled and chopped
3 ribs celery, chopped
1 carrot (large), sliced thin
3 leeks, white parts only, chopped
3 cloves garlic, minced
6 cups water
salt and pepper to taste
3 T chives, chopped, for garnish

In the melted butter, sauté onions, carrots, garlic and celery a few minutes until onion is translucent.

Transfer to a soup pot. Add all other ingredients except chives. Simmer about 1 hour or until lentils are tender.

Spoon into bowls and garnish with chopped chives.

Lentils and Chickpeas

Ingredients to serve 6:

1 cup lentils
1 large (16 oz.) can garbanzo chickpeas
1 large onion, chopped fine
1 large carrot, chopped fine
1/3 cup celery, chopped
1 t fresh garlic, minced
6 cups chicken broth
1 T poultry seasoning
1 T olive oil
salt and pepper to taste
chopped parsley for garnish

Sauté the onions, garlic and celery in the olive oil until the onions are translucent. Bring to a boil and then reduce heat and let simmer 20 minutes or until lentils are done.

Do not over-cook.

Some recipes call for adding a little lemon juice just before serving.
Garnish with chopped fresh parsley.

Lentils and Spinach Soup, Quick and Easy

Ingredients to serve 6:

4 cups chicken broth or stock (see page 105)
1 cup lentils, dried
1 cn. tomatoes (Mexican or Italian style)
1 T garlic salt
2 T onion, minced
1 pkg. frozen spinach, chopped
1 t Beau Monde or poultry seasoning
add pepper to taste

Combine all ingredients except the spinach in a soup pot, bring to a
boil, then reduce to simmer for 20 minutes. Add spinach and continue
to cook another 15 minutes. Stir together thoroughly before ladling
into soup bowls.

MUSHROOM SOUPS

Quick Cream of Mushroom Soup

Ingredients to serve 5:

2 cups fresh mushrooms
1/2 cup flour
1/8 pound butter or margarine (1/2 stick) or 4 T oil
3 cups light cream or "half and half"
1/2 t basil
salt and pepper to taste
1 T onion, chopped very fine
parsley for garnish

Chop the mushrooms (fairly large pieces), roll in flour, sauté in butter
until cooked through (do not brown). Put cream in double boiler (or
heat carefully in pan so as not to scorch), add onions, season lightly,
then add mushrooms. Do not let boil, but continue to heat until piping
hot. Garnish with parsley and serve.

Mushroom Soup with Celery and Onions #1

Ingredients to serve 8:

1-1/2 pounds fresh mushrooms
3 cups chicken broth
1/4 pound butter or margarine (1 stick) divided, or 8 T oil
1 qt. milk
1/2 cup flour
1 medium onion, chopped
3 ribs celery, chopped
1 small green (bell) pepper, seeded and chopped
1/2 t salt
1 t pepper
1 t poultry seasoning
chopped celery leaves for garnish

Using half the butter, sauté the onions, celery and pepper until the onion is translucent (a few minutes). Add the mushrooms and continue to sauté for another 5 minutes. Put contents into a soup pot; add chicken broth and simmer about 15 minutes.

Meanwhile, melt remaining butter, add flour and then add milk, slowly, stirring all the while. Bring almost to a boil, reduce heat and combine with other ingredients. Stir in seasonings. Serve piping hot.

Garnish with celery leaves.

Mushroom Soup with Celery and Onions #2

Ingredients to serve 6:

1 pound fresh mushrooms (or 1/2 pound canned) sliced
1 large onion, chopped
3 ribs celery, chopped
3 T butter, margarine or oil
4 cups chicken broth or stock (see page 105)
1 cup cream (heavy)
4 T celery leaves, chopped, for garnish
salt and pepper to taste

Sauté the mushrooms, celery and onion a few minutes until onion is translucent.

Combine in a soup pot with all other ingredients except cream, garnish and seasonings. Bring to a boil and then reduce heat to simmer for 10 minutes. Add cream and increase heat but do not let boil. Add salt and pepper to taste.

Garnish with celery leaves.

Mushroom with Lentils Soup

Ingredients to serve 6-8:

2 cups sliced, fresh mushrooms
1 small onion, chopped fine
4T butter or margarine or 4 T oil
1 rib celery, chopped fine
1/2 cup green lentils
5 cups chicken broth
2 cloves garlic, minced
1 medium carrot, chopped
1/2 t basil
salt and pepper to taste
parsley or celery leaves for garnish

Sauté onion, garlic, carrot and celery in melted butter for a few minutes or until onion is translucent.
Add mushrooms and sauté another 5 minutes.
Add chicken broth, lentils and seasonings. Bring almost to a boil, then reduce heat to simmer (about 20 minutes or until lentils are done).
Serve hot, garnished with chopped celery leaves or parsley.

ONION SOUPS*

Quick Onion Soup

Ingredients to serve 4:

3 medium to large sweet onions, peeled, sliced and broken into rings
3 cups beef broth
1 t thyme
1 t basil
1/2 t salt
1/2 t pepper
3 T parmesan cheese

Place all ingredients except the cheese in a soup kettle. Bring to a boil, then reduce heat and simmer 40 minutes. Serve hot with cheese sprinkled liberally over the surface.

*See French Onion Soup in foreign section, page 76

Onion and Garlic Soup

Ingredients to serve 8:

6 medium onions, peeled and sliced

6 heads garlic, peeled and cut into quarters

1 cup water

6 cups beef broth

1/2 cup white wine

1/2 t thyme

salt and pepper to taste

1/4 pound grated cheese of your choosing for garnish

Place garlic and onion pieces in a small baking dish. Cover with 1 cup of water and 1/2 cup wine. Bake 1 hour at 325°.

Remove from oven and place onion, liquid and garlic in a soup pot. Separate onion rings and garlic cloves with a fork. Add beef broth and spices. Bring to a boil, then reduce to simmer for 1 hour.

Serve hot with grated cheese on surface.

Garden Onion Soup

Ingredients to serve 8:

1/8 pound butter or margarine, melted (1/2 stick) or 4 T oil

2 cups leeks, white part only, sliced

6 medium onions, peeled and sliced

8 cloves of garlic, minced

6 cups beef broth (may substitute chicken)

1/2 t thyme

1 cup cream

1 t pepper

croutons or chopped leek greens for garnish

Sauté the onions and garlic in the melted butter a few minutes or until onion is translucent.

Place onion and garlic in a soup pot, add spices and beef broth. Bring to a boil, then reduce to simmer for 30 minutes.

Using a slotted spoon, set aside 1 cup of garlic and onions. Let cool, then purée the balance in batches.

Put everything back in the pot and stir in the cream. Increase heat but remove from heat just as soon as it starts to boil.

Garnish with chopped leek greens or croutons.

OLIVE SOUP

Cream of Olive Soup

Ingredients to serve 6:

1-1/2 cups black (ripe) olives, pits removed
2 avocados
3 cloves garlic, minced
1 T minced onion
2 cns. chicken broth
4 cups half and half
2 T butter or margarine or oil
1 cup dry white wine
1/2 t Tabasco sauce
salt and pepper to taste

Scoop the meat out of the avocados.
Sauté the onions and garlic in the butter or margarine.
Combine the olives, avacado meat, onion, garlic and butter just used. Purée until smooth.
Combine all ingredients in a soup pot and heat 15 minutes, but do not let boil. Serve piping hot.

PARSNIP SOUPS

Parsnips with Rutabagas

Ingredients to serve 8:

10 parsnips, scraped and sliced - about 1/4 inch
2 rutabagas, cubed - about 1/2 inch
3 carrots, sliced - about 1/4 inch
4 ribs celery, chopped
1 large onion, peeled and chopped
1 pound stew meat, cut bite-size
2 T catsup
1/2 t oregano
10 peppercorns
1/2 t salt (or to taste)
croutons for garnish

In a soup pot, cover the beef and onion with water, bring to a boil, then reduce heat and simmer 1 hour.
Add all other ingredients, cover with as much water as it takes to make the soup the consistency you like. Bring to a boil, then reduce heat to simmer for another hour or until the meat and vegetables are tender.
Garnish with croutons.

Parsnips with Cashews

Ingredients to serve 4-6:

8 parsnips, scraped and chopped
1-1/2 cups cashew halves and pieces
2 ribs celery, chopped
1 large onion, peeled and chopped
3 cloves garlic, minced
3 # 2 cns. chicken broth
1/2 t thyme
1/2 t basil
salt and pepper to taste
1 cup cream or yogurt
4 T chives, chopped, for garnish

Place all ingredients except cream and chives in a soup kettle. If all ingredients are not covered with liquid, add water. Bring to a boil then reduce heat to simmer for about 30 minutes or until parsnips are soft. Let cool, then purée in batches. Stir in cream (or yogurt) and re-heat. Garnish with chopped chives.

PEA SOUPS*

Pea Soup with Ham Bone

Ingredients to serve 6-8:

1\8 pound butter or margarine, melted (1/2 stick)
1 large onion, peeled and chopped
2 ribs celery, chopped
3 cloves garlic, minced
1 ham bone with meat on it (at least 1/2 pound of meat)
1 cup dried split peas - rinsed
3 carrots, sliced thin
5 cups chicken broth
4 tomatoes, diced
2 bay leaves
1/2 t thyme
1/2 t rosemary
1/2 t tarragon
croutons for garnish

In a soup pot, place the broth, ham bone, peas and spices. Bring to a boil, then reduce heat and simmer 45 minutes. Remove ham bone and

*See foreign section for Irish Pea Soup

let cool until meat can be cut from the bone and cubed (bite-size).

Meanwhile, in the melted butter, sauté the onions, celery and garlic a few minutes until onion is translucent.

Put all ingredients in the soup pot and continue to simmer until carrots are tender (about 20 minutes). Remove bay leaves before serving.

Garnish with croutons.

Split Pea Soup with Potatoes

Ingredients to serve 8:

1/8 pound butter or margarine, melted (1/2 stick) or 4 T oil
1 onion, peeled and chopped
2 ribs celery, chopped
2 carrots, chopped
1 pound dry split peas, rinsed
3/4 pound ham, cubed bite-size
7 cups water
2 chicken bouillon cubes
2 medium potatoes, peeled and cubed
1 t tarragon
1 t Beau Monde
1 t poultry seasoning
salt and pepper to taste
croutons for garnish

Sauté the onion and celery in the melted butter a few minutes until onion is translucent. Combine all ingredients in a soup pot and simmer 1-1/2 hours (or longer if vegetables are not tender).

Garnish with croutons.

Puréed Fresh Green Pea Soup

Ingredients to serve 4-6:

5 slices bacon, fried crisp and broken into bits (for garnish)
1/8 pound butter or margarine, melted (1/2 stick) or 4 T oil
1 medium onion, chopped fine
4 cups shelled fresh (or frozen) peas
1 rib celery, chopped
3 cups chicken broth
1 t tarragon
salt and pepper to taste

Fry or broil bacon until crisp and break into bits.

In the melted butter, sauté the onion and celery a few minutes until onion is translucent. Place all ingredients except bacon in a soup pot and simmer 5 or 6 minutes until peas are tender.

Purée soup (in batches if necessary) until smooth. Pour through a coarse sieve. Return to kettle and, using medium heat, cook until hot. Garnish bowls with bacon bits.

Creamed Pea Soup Using Canned Peas

Ingredients to serve 6:

2 cns. peas
2 cups light cream or half and half
1 small onion, chopped
1 clove garlic, chopped
2 T butter or margarine or oil
2 cups water
3 T flour (all purpose)
1/2 t nutmeg
1/2 t salt
1/2 t pepper
1 T sugar
crumbled bacon for garnish

Drain peas, reserving 1/2 cup of liquid. Purée until smooth.

Sauté the onion and garlic in the butter until onion is translucent. Stir in all seasonings, sugar and flour and add the 2 cups of water. Bring to a boil, then reduce heat and cook 2 or 3 minutes, stirring all the while. Add half and half and puréed peas. Heat thoroughly but do not let boil. Serve piping hot, garnished with crumbled bacon.

Split Pea - Bean Soup*

Ingredients to serve 20:

3 pounds split peas (dry)
1 pound navy beans (dry)
3 onions, chopped
6 ribs celery, chopped
5 bay leaves
15 peppercorns
1 T salt
1 T pepper
1 Jalapeno pepper (use 1 to 4 peppers, depending on how hot you want

it. Handle with kitchen gloves)

6 quarts water

4 pound ham with bone (more meat the better)

Make soup one day, or more, before serving (re-heat).

Use a large soup pot. Soak peas and beans in water (1 hour).

Pour off water and replace with 6 quarts fresh water.

Place all ingredients in the pot and simmer until peas and beans are very soft. When meat is about ready to fall off the bone, remove ham from kettle, let cool to handle and break or cut lean meat (discard fat and bone) into small pieces. Return meat to kettle. If vegetables are not soft, continue to cook until they are.

Refrigerate until next day.

Remove bay leafs before serving.

Option: change the ratio of beans to peas; half and half for example.

*Courtesy Harold Wolfe, St. Cloud, Minnesota

POTATO SOUPS*

Potato with Onion

Ingredients to serve 4:

2 cups potatoes, peeled and chopped quite fine

1 small onion, chopped fine

1 rib celery, chopped fine

1 clove garlic, chopped fine

3 medium leeks, chopped (both white and green parts)

1 small carrot, sliced thin (optional)

1/4 pound butter or margarine, melted (1 stick) or 8 T oil

2-1/2 cups chicken broth

1/2 cup cream

1 t poultry seasoning

2 T chopped parsley (either stir into soup or use as garnish)

Melt butter and sauté potatoes, onion, celery, carrot and garlic for a few minutes or until onion pieces are translucent. Add leeks and all other ingredients except parsley. Cook over low heat until potatoes are soft. Serve hot. Either stir in parsley or use as garnish on surface.

See page 82 for Welsh Potato Soup

Potato with Corn

Ingredients to serve 6:

2 medium potatoes, chopped
1 carrot, chopped
2 cups fresh corn (may substitute whole kernel in the can)
1 clove garlic, minced
1/4 pound butter or margarine (1 stick) or 8 T oil
2 ribs celery, chopped
1 small jar pimentos
1/2 t basil
2 T chopped green pepper
4 cups chicken broth
1 t poultry seasoning
salt and pepper to taste

Using the melted butter, sauté the onion, celery, green pepper and garlic a few minutes until onion is translucent. Add corn and potatoes and continue to sauté until potatoes soften. (If corn is already cooked, do not sauté).

Add other ingredients except broth. Continue to heat and stir about 2 minutes. Add broth; let simmer 20 minutes or until all vegetables are soft.

Deer Camp Potato Soup

Ingredients to serve 8:

5 potatoes (medium), peeled, cooked and diced
2 ribs celery, chopped
2 carrots, sliced thin
1 large onion, chopped
2 cloves garlic, minced
3 T flour
1/8 pound butter or margarine (1/2 stick) melted, or 4 T oil
1-1/2 quarts milk
1/2 t basil
1/2 t thyme
1 bay leaf
2 chicken or beef bouillon cubes
1/2 t salt (to taste)
1 t pepper (to taste)
1/4 pound cheddar cheese, grated and shredded (as garnish)

Cook potatoes in salted water until easily penetrated with a fork.
Sauté the celery, onion, carrots and garlic in melted butter a couple of

minutes or until onion is translucent. Stir in flour and slowly add milk.
Add all other ingredients except cheese and potatoes.

Cook about 20 minutes (stirring regularly) or until soup starts to thicken.

Add the pre-cooked, diced potatoes. Simmer another 20 minutes or until piping hot. Remove bay leaf. Spoon shredded cheese on top of each serving.

Quick and Rich Potato Soup

Ingredients to serve 6:

1 medium onion, chopped
2 ribs celery, chopped
1 clove garlic, minced
3 cups chicken broth
3 cups potatoes, peeled and diced
2 cups half and half or heavier cream
1/2 t oregano
1/2 t pepper
chopped chives or parsley for garnish

In a soup pot, place all the ingredients except the cream. Bring to a boil then reduce heat and cook for 15 to 20 minutes or until potatoes are soft. Add the cream and continue to cook until piping hot but do not let boil. Serve with choice of garnish.

If you prefer, you may purée the soup before you add the cream. Let cool first, however, so that the soup may be handled safely.

Potato Soup with Spinach

Ingredients to serve 4:

2 medium potatoes, peeled and diced
2 cups frozen spinach (or fresh leaves) packed
1 onion, peeled and chopped
3 cups water
1 cup milk
1/2 t curry powder
salt and pepper to taste
garnish with 4 t chopped chives

Cook the diced potatoes and onion in the water until soft (15-20 minutes).

Meanwhile, chop the spinach (unless frozen is already chopped).

Let potatoes cool. In a blender, purée potatoes (with water) spinach and onion. Return to soup kettle and add all other ingredients except chives. Bring to a boil, then reduce heat to simmer for 20 minutes. Garnish with chives.

Baked Potato Soup

Ingredients to serve 8:

5 medium baked potatoes (skin may be left on) diced
1 medium onion, chopped
2 ribs celery, chopped
1 clove garlic, minced
1 cn. cream of chicken soup
1 cn. cream of celery soup
2 cns. water
1 cup cream
1/8 pound butter or margarine (1/2 stick) or 4 T oil
6 slices bacon, fried or broiled crisp and broken into bits
1/4 pound cheddar cheese, shredded or grated
salt and pepper to taste

Bake potatoes, let cook, cut into small chunks
Sauté the onion, celery and garlic in the melted butter a few minutes or until onion is translucent. Combine all ingredients (except bacon and cheese) in a soup pot. Simmer over low heat for 20 minutes; do not boil. Meanwhile, fry or broil bacon and break into bits. Serve soup piping hot with cheese and bacon on surface as garnish.

Potato with Tomato

Ingredients to serve 6-8:

5 medium potatoes, peeled and diced
3 cns. Italian style tomatoes
1 onion, chopped
2 ribs celery, chopped
2 cloves garlic, minced
2 bay leaves
1/2 cup cream
1/2 t sage
1/2 t oregano
1/8 pound butter or margarine (1/2 stick) or 4 T oil
2 T catsup
enough water to cover potatoes plus 4 cups
parsley or celery leaves for garnish

In the melted butter, sauté onion, celery and garlic a few minutes until onion is translucent.

In a soup pot, cover the chopped potatoes with water and cook (boil) until potatoes are soft. Discard water. Add all other ingredients (including 4 cups of water and liquid in cns. of tomatoes) and bring to a boil. Reduce heat immediately and let simmer about 10 minutes. Remove bay leaves. Serve piping hot.

Garnish with parsley or celery leaves.

Potato Soup with Carrots and a hint of Orange

Ingredients to serve 6:

2 large potatoes, peeled and diced

4 carrots, sliced thin

2 cns. chicken broth

2 cns. water

1 orange (juice of and rind grated)

1 bay leaf

1 T brown sugar

1 cup cream

1 t Tabasco sauce

salt and pepper

In a soup pot, combine the diced potatoes, sliced carrots, chicken broth, water, sugar, Tabasco and bay leaf. Bring to a boil, then reduce heat to simmer and cook for 20 to 30 minutes or until vegetables are tender. Let cool to handle safely. Remove and discard bay leaf. Add the grated orange rind and juice.

Purée the soup in batches; return to kettle.

Add cream and re-heat until piping hot but do not let boil. Season to taste.

Potato Soup with Bacon or Ham

Ingredients to serve 8:

5 large potatoes, peeled and diced

6 pieces bacon*

6 cups chicken broth or stock

2 onions, peeled and chopped

4 T butter, margarine or oil

3 leeks, sliced, including green parts
1 bay leaf
1 cup cream
1/2 cup white wine
1 t coriander
salt and pepper to taste

Sauté the onion and leeks in the butter a few minutes until translucent. Place in a soup pot with all ingredients except the cream and wine. Bring to a boil, then reduce heat to simmer and cook for 30 minutes or until the potatoes are soft. Let cool for safe handling. Remove bay leaf.

Meanwhile, broil or fry the bacon until crisp. Break into small pieces and set aside.

Purée the soup. Return to the kettle and re-heat.

Serve with crumbled bacon for garnish
chunks of ham may be substituted

Sweet Potato Soup

Ingredients to serve 6:

3 large sweet potatoes
1 carrot, scraped and sliced
1 rib celery, chopped
1 onion, chopped
1 cn. lima beans, drained
1 t garlic salt
1 T brown sugar
1 t cinnamon
4 cups water
add pepper to taste
parsley for garnish

Combine all ingredients in a soup pot. Bring to a boil, then reduce heat to simmer and cook for 40 minutes or until all vegetables are tender.

Option: let cool and purée in batches and re-heat.

Add parsley for garnish.

PUMPKIN AND SQUASH SOUPS

Pumpkin Soup in the Shell

Ingredients to serve 6-8:

1 large pumpkin (6-8 pounds)
1 onion, peeled and chopped
6 cups chicken broth
2 hard apples, peeled, cored and diced
2 carrots, chopped
1 potato, peeled and cubed
8 slices bacon, fried or broiled until crisp and broken into bits
1/2 t rosemary
1/2 t basil
1 t cumin
croutons for garnish

Remove top (about 1/4) of pumpkin. Scoop out seeds and stringy pulp. Replace top, set in a baking pan and bake in 350° oven 1 hour or until meat can be easily scooped out (but not soft). Scoop out meat, leaving about a half-inch shell. Cut pumpkin meat into smaller than bite-size pieces.

Place all ingredients in a soup pot. Bring to a boil, then reduce and simmer for 30 minutes or until all vegetables are soft.

Pour pot's contents into the pumpkin shell, set in a baking pan and return to oven. Bake 20 minutes. Serve with croutons.

Squash Soup

Ingredients to serve 4-6:

1 4 pound squash of your choosing
1-1/2 cups cream
2 cups chicken broth
2 T brown sugar
1/2 t sage
1/2 t nutmeg
salt and pepper to taste
marshmallows for garnish

Cut squash in half. Scoop out seeds and stringy pulp. Cover each half with foil and bake in a 300° oven about 1 hour or until meat is soft. (May use microwave to save time).

Scoop meat out of skin; discard skin. Mash pieces of squash with a large spoon. Place squash in soup pot. Add all ingredients. Bring to a boil, then reduce heat and simmer 20 minutes. If soup is "lumpy", force through a coarse sieve. Serve hot.

Float a marshmallow in each cup of soup.

Pumpkin Soup

Ingredients to serve 6:

3 cups cooked pumpkin (may be canned)
1 onion, peeled and chopped
1 rib celery, chopped
4 cups chicken broth
2 T orange juice
1 cup cream
1 T sugar
1 T brown sugar
2 T butter or margarine or oil
salt and pepper to taste
1/2 t ginger

Sauté onion and celery a couple of minutes or until onion is translucent.

Place all ingredients in a soup pot. Bring to a boil, then reduce to simmer and cook 20 minutes.

Optional garnish: float a marshmallow in each bowl.

Creamy Pumpkin Soup

Ingredients to serve 6:

2 cups canned or cooked pumpkin meat
2 cups diced potatoes
1 medium onion, chopped
1 clove garlic, minced
2 cns. chicken broth
2 cups half and half
1/2 t salt
1/2 t pepper
1 t nutmeg (ground)
sour cream and chopped parsley for garnish

Sauté onion and garlic in butter or margarine. Place in a soup pot and add potatoes, pumpkin and broth. Cook until potatoes are tender. Let cool so that it is safe to handle. Purée in batches.

Return to pot and add all other ingredients. Heat thoroughly but do not let boil (about 20 minutes).

Garnish servings with dollops of sour cream sprinkled with chopped parsley.

Quick Pumpkin with Apple Soup

Ingredients to serve 4:

1 cn. (15 oz.) pumpkin
1 cn. (14 oz.) chicken broth
1 cup apple sauce
1/2 t allspice (powder)
1 t cinnamon
salt and pepper to taste

If the canned pumpkin is not already of purée texture, purée until smooth.

Place all ingredients (except salt and pepper) in a soup pot and heat thoroughly, stirring occasionally. Add salt and pepper to taste.

Zucchini Soup

Ingredients to serve 4:

1/8 pound butter or margarine (1/2 stick), melted or 4 T oil
4 average size zucchini squash, cubed
3 cups water
2 ribs celery, chopped
1 cup heavy cream or yogurt
1 t basil
1/2 t thyme
salt and pepper to taste
parsley flakes for garnish

Sauté the celery and zucchini in batches, about 1/3 at a time for about 2 or 3 minutes or until squash starts to change color (golden).

Place all ingredients except cream (or yogurt) and parsley in a soup kettle. Bring to a boil, then reduce heat to simmer for about 20 minutes or until squash is tender.

Stir in cream (or yogurt), continue to cook (but not boil) another 5 minutes so that soup is heated throughout.

Garnish with parsley flakes.

Option: Soup could be cooled and then puréed (in batches). Add cream or yogurt after blending. Re-heat.

RADISH SOUP

Cream of Radish Soup

Ingredients to serve 4:

12-15 radishes (variety of your choosing) sliced or chopped
2 cns. chicken broth
1 cn. water
2 cns. half and half
1 onion, chopped
1 t soy sauce
1 bay leaf
1/4 t Tabasco sauce
parsley flakes for garnish

Place the radishes, soup, water, onion and bay leaf in a soup pot. Bring to a boil, then reduce heat to simmer. Cook 15 minutes or until radishes start to soften. Remove from heat and let cool.

Remove the solids with a slotted spoon. Discard the bay leaf. Place the solid ingredients in a blender along with about a cup of the liquid. Purée until smooth. Return to the pot with the other ingredients and heat thoroughly without bringing it to a boil.

Garnish with parsley flakes.

SPINACH SOUPS

Spinach with Cheese

Ingredients to serve 6:

1/8 pound butter or margarine, melted (1/2 stick) or 4 T oil
2 medium onions, peeled, sliced and broken into rings
5 cups spinach leaves, cut-up (not chopped too small)
4 cups chicken broth
8 oz. cheese, grated (Monterey Jack, or Swiss, or cheddar or Roquefort)
2 ribs celery, chopped
1/2 cup white wine
3 tomatoes, diced
1 cup heavy cream
1/2 t thyme
1/2 t rosemary
6 slices bacon, fried or broiled crisp and broken into bits for garnish

Sauté the celery and onions a few minutes until onion is translucent. Save butter and transfer onions and celery to a soup pot.

Add all other ingredients except spinach, cream and tomatoes. Bring to

a boil, reduce heat and simmer until cheese is melted (stir regularly).
Meanwhile, broil or fry bacon until crisp. Cool and break into bits for garnish.

Sauté the spinach in the left-over butter just until it begins to wilt (about 2 minutes).

Add spinach, cream and tomatoes to soup pot. Continue cooking about 5 minutes or until soup is thoroughly heated.

Garnish bowls with bacon bits.

This soup can be puréed.

Spinach with Tortellini Soup

Ingredients to serve 6:

1 pkg. frozen spinach, thawed, drained and chopped

1/2 pound cheese tortellini

1 onion, chopped

1 clove garlic, minced

2 T butter, margarine or oil

3 cups chicken broth

1 cn. Italian style tomatoes

salt and pepper to taste

Sauté the onion and garlic in butter or oil until onion is translucent.

In a soup pot, combine the onion, garlic broth and tortellini. Bring to a boil, then reduce heat and simmer for 10 minutes or until the tortellini is tender.

Add the spinach and tomatoes and continue to cook until thoroughly heated, (10-15 minutes). Season to taste.

Spinach with Tomato

Ingredients to serve 6:

1/8 pound butter or margarine (1/2 stick) or 4 T oil

1 onion, peeled and chopped

3 cloves garlic, minced

1 rib celery, chopped

2 cns. tomatoes, diced

1 small cn. tomato soup

2 cns. water

2 T tomato paste

2 T catsup

1 pkg. frozen spinach, chopped
1/2 t basil
1/2 t oregano
1 bay leaf (remove after cooking)

Sauté the onion, garlic and celery in the melted butter.

Combine all ingredients, except the spinach, in a soup pot. Bring to a boil then reduce heat to simmer. Cook 20 minutes.

Add spinach, cook another 2 or 3 minutes, stirring all the while.

TOMATO SOUPS

Fresh Garden Tomato

Ingredients to serve 4-6:

4 large tomatoes, peeled and diced
1/8 pound butter or margarine, (1/2 stick) or 4 T oil
8 leeks, chopped - white part only
2 ribs celery, chopped
2 cloves garlic, minced
4 T tomato paste
2 cups water
2 cups chicken broth
2 T catsup
6 drops Tabasco sauce
4 T chives, chopped for garnish (or parsley)

Sauté the onions, celery and garlic a few minutes or until onion is translucent.

Combine all ingredients in a soup pot (except the garnish). Bring to a boil, then reduce heat to simmer and cook 20 minutes.

Garnish with chives or parsley.

Quick Tomato Bisque

Ingredients to serve 6:

2 cns. stewed tomatoes
2 cns. diced tomatoes
1 cn. tomato sauce
1 T tomato paste
2 cups water
1 pint cream
1 chicken bouillon cube

salt and pepper to taste
chopped chives for garnish

Combine all ingredients in a soup pot. Bring to a low boil and quickly reduce to simmer, stirring intermittently. Cook for 20 minutes. Garnish with chives.

Creamy Tomato Soup

Ingredients to serve 8:

1/8 pound butter or margarine (1/2 stick) or 4 T oil
1 cn. diced tomatoes (28 oz.)
2 cups tomato juice
1 large onion, peeled and chopped
2 cloves garlic, peeled and minced
3 carrots, scraped and chopped
2 ribs celery, chopped .
1/2 cup water
3 T flour
1 T basil, dried
4 cups half and half
seasoned croutons for garnish

Sauté the onion, celery, garlic and carrots for 2 or 3 minutes or until onion is translucent. Transfer to a soup pot.
Add all other ingredients except the flour and water. Heat until bubbly - do not boil - reduce heat to simmer. Cook 30 minutes or until celery and carrots are soft.
Combine the flour and water; stir until smooth. Add to the soup, stirring all the while. Continue to heat another 5 minutes.
Garnish with croutons.

Really Creamy Tomato Soup

Ingredients to serve 6:

4 cups diced fresh tomatoes (or canned tomatoes)
1 medium onion, chopped
2 ribs celery, chopped
2 garlic cloves, minced
2 medium carrots, sliced thin or chopped
3 T butter or margarine or oil
3 cups water
1 cup white wine

2 cups heavy cream
1 t oregano
1/4 t pepper
croutons for garnish

Sauté the onion, celery, garlic and carrots in the butter a few minutes or until onion is translucent (do not let burn). Place in a soup pot.

Add 2 cups of water, 1 cup of wine and seasonings. (If you prefer to retain some of the alcohol in the soup, add wine at the end). Bring to a boil, then reduce to simmer and cook until the carrots are soft. Let cool.

When cool enough to handle safely, purée in batches. Return to soup pot.

Add cream and more water if the soup is too thick. Re-heat but do not let boil.

Serve piping hot garnished with croutons.

Tomato with Onion and Celery

Ingredients to serve 4-6:

1 onion, peeled and chopped

2 ribs celery, chopped

1 medium potato, peeled and diced

2 cloves garlic, minced

1/8 pound butter or margarine (1/2 stick) or 4 t oil

2-1/2 cups diced tomatoes

1 t oregano

1 t basil

3 cups chicken broth

salt and pepper to taste

3 t chopped chives or parsley for garnish

Sauté the onion, celery and garlic in the melted butter until onion is translucent. (2 or 3 minutes).

Set aside 1 cup of diced tomatoes.

Place all ingredients except the cup of tomatoes in a soup kettle; bring to a boil, then reduce to simmer. Cook 20 minutes or until potato is soft. Cool until easy to handle.

Purée in batches and return to kettle. Add cup of uncooked tomatoes. Re-heat.

Garnish with chives or parsley.

TURTLE SOUPS

Traditional Turtle Soup

Ingredients to serve 8:

2 pounds turtle meat, cubed bite-size

1/2 cup flour

cooking oil

seasoning (salt, pepper and your favorite soup or stew seasoning-such as Beau Monde)

1 large onion, chopped

other vegetables of your choice, such as:

1 cup celery, cut into 1/2 to 1 inch pieces

4 medium potatoes, cut bite-size

1 large can tomatoes (or fresh tomatoes, diced)

4 large carrots, sliced thick

1 medium rutabaga, cut bite-size

2 cubes beef or chicken bouillon—or use soup starter according to the recipe on the package for 2 quarts of water

2 qts. water

Season the cut up meat with salt and pepper, roll in flour and brown in a heavy skillet over medium heat (in cooking oil).

Place the browned turtle in a kettle or crock pot, cover with 2 quarts of water. Let simmer for one hour. After the first 30 minutes, add the chopped onion, bouillon cubes and any other seasonings you like in soup or stew.

After the hour, add the vegetables and let simmer for a second hour or until the vegetables are well done and turtle is tender (relatively!)

Turtle Gumbo

Ingredients to serve 8:

2 pounds turtle meat, cut bite-size

1/2 cup flour

1 stick butter or margarine or 8 T oil

1 cn. mushroom pieces (or 1/2 pound fresh)

1 clove garlic, diced very fine

1 green pepper, chopped

1 medium onion, chopped

1 cup celery, chopped

2 #2 cns. tomato sauce and 1 small cn. tomato purée

3 cups water

1/2 cup cooking wine (red)

seasoning-salt and pepper plus 4 drops Tabasco sauce

4 cups cooked rice

Lightly season the turtle meat with salt and pepper and dredge in flour. Fry in cooking oil and margarine (or butter). Use a heavy skillet and medium heat.

Add onion, celery and garlic. Sauté until onion is translucent. Add 3 cups water; bring to a boil; reduce heat to simmer; cook 1 hour.

Add all other ingredients; simmer 1 hour or until meat is tender.

Serve over rice.

VEGETABLE SOUPS

Vegetarian Minestrone

Ingredients to serve 10:

1/8 pound butter or margarine (1/2 stick), melted or 4 T oil

2 ribs celery, chopped

2 cloves garlic, minced

2 medium carrots, sliced thin

2 medium onions, peeled and sliced and broken into rings

2 cups green beans, cut into 1-1/2 inch pieces

1 cn. white beans of your choice

2 medium potatoes, peeled and diced

4 cups chicken broth

3 cups water

5 tomatoes, diced (may substitute canned)

1 medium zucchini, diced

2 cups coarsely shredded cabbage

1/2 t salt

1 t pepper (or to taste)

2 bay leaves

1 t crushed basil

1 T catsup

Sauté (in butter) onions, celery and garlic a few minutes or until onion is translucent. Place in soup pot and add all other ingredients except cabbage. Bring to a boil, then reduce heat and simmer 40 minutes. Add cabbage and continue to simmer another 20 minutes. Remove bay leaves.

Minestrone with Beef

Ingredients to serve 10:

1/8 pound butter or margarine (1/2 stick) or 4 T oil

3 cloves garlic, minced

1 large onion, chopped

2 ribs celery, chopped

1-1/2 pounds stew meat, cut into bite-size cubes

7 cups water

3 beef bouillon cubes

1 cn. white beans

1 cn. garbonzo chickpeas

1/2 cup lentils

2 carrots, sliced thin

5 tomatoes, diced

1 box (8 oz.) shell macaroni

2 potatoes, peeled and cubed

1 t oregano

1 t thyme

1 t basil

2 bay leaves

1 t pepper

1/2 t salt

4 T flour (in which to roll beef cubes)

Cook macaroni separately per instructions on box.

Melt butter and sauté beef cubes (rolled in flour), onions, celery and garlic a few minutes or until onion is translucent and beef is browned - stir and toss so as not to burn.

Place above ingredients, the water, spices and bouillon cubes in a soup pot. Bring to a boil, then reduce heat. Cook until beef is tender (about 1-1/2 hours).

Add all remaining ingredients except macaroni and continue to simmer for 20 minutes. Add macaroni and continue to cook until carrots and potatoes are soft.

Remove bay leaves before serving.

Vegetable Soup with Ham

Ingredients to serve 6-8:

1 onion, chopped

1 clove garlic, minced

1 spear celery, chopped

1 carrot, sliced thin
1/8 pound butter or margarine (1/2 stick) or 4 T oil
1 cup diced potatoes
1/3 cup rice
2 cups chicken broth or stock (page 105)
2 cups water
1 cup half and half
1/2 t thyme
1/2 t basil
1 bay leaf
salt and pepper to taste
1-1/2 cups ham, diced and pre-cooked
2 cups spinach leaves, chopped
chopped parsley for garnish

Sauté the onion, garlic, celery and carrot in butter a few minutes or until onion is translucent. Place in a soup pot.

Add all other ingredients except the spinach; bring to a boil, then reduce heat to simmer. Cook until rice is flowered and carrots and potatoes are soft (15-20 minutes). Add spinach and cook another 2 minutes.

Remove bay leaf before serving.

Garnish with parsley.

Quick Vegetable Beef Soup*

Ingredients to serve 4:

1/8 pound butter or margarine, melted (1/2 stick) or 4 T oil
1/2 pound lean ground beef
2 cups hot water
3/4 cup chopped celery
3/4 cup diced potatoes
1 t salt
1/4 t pepper
1/2 bay leaf, crumbled
1/8 t dried, sweet basil
1/4 t chives, chopped
1/8 t garlic powder
1/8 t dried thyme
1/2 Jalapeno pepper, seeded and chopped (use kitchen gloves)
1 16 oz. cn. tomatoes
2 carrots, thinly sliced

Brown the crumbled ground beef in the butter or oil.

Place all the contents in a soup pot, bring to a boil, then reduce to simmer for 30 minutes or until vegetables are tender.

*Courtesy Barbara Olson, Anchorage

Cheesy Garden Chowder

Ingredients to serve 6-8:

1 medium onion, chopped
2 ribs celery, chopped
1 medium zucchini, sliced thin
3 T butter or margarine or oil
4 medium tomatoes, diced (may substitute canned)
2 cups fresh corn (may substitute frozen)
1 cup fresh peas (may substitute frozen)
3 cups chicken broth or stock (page 105)
2 cups milk
1 bay leaf
1 t basil
2 cups shredded cheddar cheese
salt and pepper to taste
chopped chives or parsley for garnish

Sauté the onion, celery and zucchini a few minutes until squash is soft. Place in a soup pot.
Add all ingredients except milk, tomatoes and cheese. Bring to a boil then reduce heat and cook 20 minutes or until corn is tender. Add milk, tomatoes and cheese and continue to cook (not boil) until cheese is melted. Stir occasionally.
Remove bay leaf before serving.
Garnish with chives or parsley.

WILD RICE SOUPS

Wild Rice with Chicken

Ingredients to serve 6:

1/3 cup uncooked wild rice (between 1/3 and 1/2 cup)
2 cups cooked chicken, cubed (bite-size)
2 T chopped onions
2 T chopped celery
1 cup fresh mushrooms (or 1/2 cup canned)
1 cup chicken broth
1/2 cup flour
1/2 t poultry seasoning
1/2 t garlic salt
1/2 t crushed basil
1/2 t pepper

1 qt. milk (may use half cream)
1/2 cup shredded or grated cheddar cheese
1/8 pound butter or margarine (1/2 stick) or 4 T oil
parsley sprigs for garnish

Prepare wild rice in a sauce pan. Cover with a generous amount of water. Bring to a boil, reduce heat and let simmer for 1 hour or until rice is flowered out. Stir occasionally. Do not let dry out; add water if necessary.

When rice is ready, combine the melted butter, milk, seasonings and flour (the flour will mix better if you first stir it into about a cup of the milk). Use a 2 quart or larger soup pot. Simmer (do not let boil) about 20 minutes; stir regularly. When it starts to thicken, add all other ingredients. Simmer on low heat about 30 minutes; then increase heat for a few minutes but do not let boil. Serve piping hot.

Garnish with parsley.

Wild Rice with Mushrooms

Ingredients to serve 6:

1/3 cup uncooked wild rice
1 cns. Cream of Mushroom soup
1/3 pound fresh mushrooms (or one 4 oz. cn.)
1/2 cup chopped celery
1/2 cup chopped onion
1 carrot, sliced thin
2 cups half and half
1/2 t rosemary
1/2 t thyme
4 slices bacon, broiled and cut into small pieces
1/8 pound butter or margarine (1/2 stick) or 4 T oil
salt and pepper to taste
parsley flakes for garnish

In a sauce pan, cover the wild rice with a generous amount of water. Let simmer for an hour or until the kernels have well flowered. Stir occasionally; if it dries out, add water.

Sauté the onion, celery and carrot until the onion pieces are translucent.

Broil or fry the bacon until not quite crisp. Cut into small pieces.

Combine all ingredients except parsley in a soup pot; bring to a low boil; reduce heat and let simmer 1 hour. Serve hot, garnished with the parsley flakes.

Wild Rice with Vegetables and Beef

Ingredients for 16:

5 to 6 pound soup bone (shank with about 1 to 2 pounds meat on the bone)
2 large onions, sliced
3 large carrots, sliced
2 cups celery, chopped
1/2 cup parsley, chopped
3 large potatoes, cubed
1 #2 cn. tomatoes
1/2 cup uncooked wild rice, well washed
1/3 cup catsup
2 bay leaves
1 T Beau Monde seasoning
salt and pepper to taste

Simmer wild rice in water until flowered.

Meanwhile, using a large soup kettle, cover soup bone with one gallon water. Add seasonings and let simmer 1 hour. Add all other ingredients and let simmer 3 more hours. Remove bay leaves.

Remove soup bone and let cool enough to handle.

Cut meat from bone into bite-size chunks. Return meat to soup kettle. Heat a few more minutes and serve.

Wild Rice Scotch Broth with Venison

Ingredients to serve 8:

2 pounds venison roast or stew meat, cubed into bite-size chunks
2 onions, sliced
2 carrots, sliced
2 T parsley, chopped
2 potatoes, cubed
1/2 cup wild rice, uncooked
1 bay leaf
8 peppercorns
salt and pepper to taste
parsley sprigs for garnish

Cover cubed meat with 2 quarts of water, bring to boil, then let simmer one hour. Add all other ingredients. Cover and let simmer 3 additional hours over low heat. Remove bay leaf.

Garnish with parsley sprigs.

Creamy Wild Rice Soup*

Ingredients to serve 6:

1 cup wild rice
4 cns. low fat chicken broth
1-1/2 cups sliced carrots
1-1/2 cups bite-size cooked chicken breast
1 bay leaf
3/4 stick butter
flour
1 pt. whipping cream
pepper to taste
water to cover wild rice (about 1 quart)
sliced almonds for garnish

In a soup pot, cover the wild rice with about 1 quart of water. Bring to a boil, then reduce heat to simmer and cook until half-done. You may need to add water while it is cooking. Drain the rice.

Bring the chicken broth to a boil; add rice, carrots, chicken and the bay leaf and reduce heat to boil lightly until the rice and the carrots are done.

In a small pan, melt the butter and stir in enough flour to make a smooth, thick paste. Add to the broth mixture. Continue to boil for several minutes. Reduce heat so that it is no longer boiling. Add the whipping cream and continue to cook until fully heated, do not boil. Remove the bay leaf.

Add pepper to taste - serve with sliced almonds on top.

*Courtesy Nancy Allen, Bemidji, Mn

Wash Day Soup

A couple of generations ago, before there were automatic washers and dryers, washing clothes was an all-day chore. In our home, washday always fell on Monday. Because it took so long to wash clothes, the noon meal had to be simple. My mother always made soup, and this was one of our favorites.

Ingredients to serve 10: (Mother usually refrigerated half for later in the week)

2 pounds stew meat, cubed (beef, ham, or big game)
1/2 cup wild rice, uncooked
1/2 cup split peas
1 large carrot, sliced
1 large potato, cubed
1 large onion, sliced

1 large turnip, sliced
1 cup celery, chopped
1 cup cabbage, shredded or cut (not too fine)
1 bay leaf
salt and pepper to taste

Using a large soup kettle, cover meat with 3 quarts of water. If you suspect meat may be tough, let simmer one hour with seasonings before adding other ingredients.

Add all ingredients except cabbage and let simmer 3 hours.

Add cabbage during last 30-40 minutes.

Remove bay leaf before serving.

Part II
SOUPS FROM FOREIGN LANDS

African Creamy Peanut Soup*

Ingredients to serve 6:

2 T oil
1/2 cup chopped celery (fine)
1 large onion, chopped fine
6 cups chicken broth
1-1/2 cups peanut butter (creamy style)
2 cups cream
salt and pepper to taste

Sauté the onion and celery in the oil.
Combine with the broth in a large sauce pan. Bring to a boil, then reduce heat to simmer. Add peanut butter and stir until blended.
Add salt and pepper to taste.
Strain out solids and discard. Add cream, slowly, stirring it in. Stir over low heat for 2 or 3 minutes but do not let boil.

*Courtesy Seth Ashiama, Ghana

Bean Soup from South Africa

Ingredients to serve 6:

3 cups dried brown beans, washed
5 cups water
1 onion, chopped
1 carrot, scraped and sliced
4 tomatoes, chopped
4 T butter, margarine or oil
2 pounds beef shortribs, including the bones
1 T sugar

1/2 t nutmeg
1 t salt
1 t pepper
2 T parsley, chopped
parsley sprigs for garnish

Sauté the onion and carrots a few minutes until onion is translucent.
Place the beans and water in a soup pot. Bring to a boil, then reduce
heat to simmer for 30 minutes. Add the shortribs and all other
ingredients to the soup pot; bring to a boil, then reduce heat to simmer
for 2 hours or until the beans and meat are both tender.

Remove the ribs and let both the meat and the soup cool so they may
be safely handled. Purée two-thirds of the soup in batches. Remove the
meat from the bones and cut into bite-size pieces. Discard the bones.

Return the meat and the puréed soup to the pot. If it is too thick, add
water until you are satisfied it is the right consistency.

Bring to a boil, then reduce heat to simmer for 10 minutes or until
piping hot. Add more salt and pepper if necessary.

Garnish with parsley sprigs.

Chinese Egg Drop Soup

Ingredients to serve 4:

4 cups water
2 T instant chicken bouillon
1 large egg, beaten lightly
1/2 t salt
1/2 t white pepper
2 T corn starch
3 T water
4 t chives, chopped, for garnish

Bring the water to boiling; reduce heat to simmer. Add chicken
bouillon, salt and pepper.

Stir together the corn starch and water; stir into soup.

Beat the egg lightly. Add it slowly to the soup, stirring all the while
with a fork until the egg becomes stringy.

Stir a little as the soup is ladled into the bowls so that some of the egg
will be in each. Garnish each bowl with the chopped chives.

Danish Beer Soup

Ingredients to serve 4-6:

3 cups cooked egg noodles
1/4 pound butter or margarine (1 stick) cut into half-inch chunks
2 T cinnamon
salt and pepper to taste
3 cns. beer of your choosing (not refrigerated)
crouton-size pieces of dark rye bread for garnish

As soon as the cooked egg noodles have been drained, stir in the butter slices until they melt. Stir in the pepper, salt and cinnamon. Cover the noodles with the beer. Heat until hot but do not let boil. Garnish with bits of rye bread.

Finnish Moijakka

Ingredients to serve 8:

2 pounds stew meat, cubed - bite-size
1 large onion, chopped
3 ribs celery, chopped
12 peppercorns
6 medium potatoes, peeled and chopped
1 medium rutabaga, chopped
1 medium head cabbage, shredded
6 carrots, sliced
1 turnip, chopped
1 beef bouillon cube dissolved in 1 cup water
1/2 t salt
oil to brown meat

Brown the stew meat. Cover with water and simmer until meat starts to tenderize (about 30-40 minutes). Meanwhile, chop vegetables - not too small. Add celery, carrots, onion and peppercorns and let simmer another 30 minutes.
Add all other ingredients except cabbage and cover with water. Simmer until potatoes, rutabaga and turnip pieces are tender.
Add cabbage and simmer another 10 minutes.

French Onion Soup

Ingredients to serve 4:

6 cups beef stock (page 106)
6 peppercorns
4 medium onions (preferably yellow), sliced thin and broken into rings
3 T butter or margarine or oil
1/4 cup dry red wine or cooking sherry
4 slices Swiss cheese
4 pieces round toast, cut to fit easily into the bowls

Place the beef stock and one-half of the onion rings in a large soup pot and bring to a boil. Reduce heat and let simmer. Meanwhile, melt the butter in a skillet and sauté the rest of the onion rings until translucent. Add onions to the pot and let simmer 60 minutes. Add sherry or wine and let simmer another 30 minutes or until onions are tender.

Ladle soup into 4 oven-proof bowls. Float a piece of round toast in each. Lay a piece of Swiss cheese on top of each piece of toast. Place under broiler (briefly) until cheese is melted (starts to brown).

Grecian Lemon Soup

Ingredients to serve 6:

1/3 cup rice, uncooked
6 cups chicken broth
4 eggs - yolks only
2 T grated lemon rind
2 T lemon juice, fresh
salt - just a dash
thin lemon slices for garnish

Place the chicken broth in a soup kettle and bring to a boil. Add rice and cook until done (about 20 minutes).

Meanwhile, beat egg yolks in a small bowl; add lemon rind and juice; pour into broth. Simmer about 5 minutes, stirring occasionally.

Float a lemon slice in each bowl for garnish.

Pumpkin Soup from India

Ingredients to serve 6:

2 cups pumpkin meat, small cubes
5 cups chicken broth
2 onions, peeled and chopped
4 T oil
2 T flour
2 cups milk
1/2 t powdered curry
1/2 t nutmeg
salt to taste
pepper to taste
heavy cream and paprika for garnish

Sauté the onion in the oil until pieces are translucent. Remove from heat and stir in the flour until smooth. Place in a soup pot.

Add all other ingredients except garnish. Bring to a boil, then reduce heat to simmer for about 30 minutes or until pumpkin is soft. Remove from heat and let cool.

Strain everything through a strainer - use force. Discard the pulp.

Return soup to pot and bring to a boil; reduce heat and let simmer 10 minutes or until piping hot.

Garnish with a tablespoon of heavy cream and sprinkle with paprika.

Irish Split Pea Soup

Ingredients to serve 6:

1-1/2 cups split peas (cleaned, picked through and rinsed)
1 ham hock or 1 cup diced, pre-cooked ham
5 cups chicken broth
1 onion, chopped
2 T cooking oil (traditionally bacon drippings)
2 stalks celery, chopped fine
2 potatoes, peeled and diced
1 carrot, diced
1 T flour
3 bay leaves
1/2 t savory

1/4 t ground cloves
salt and freshly ground pepper to taste
parsley flakes to garnish (or chopped fresh)

Sauté the onion, celery and garlic in oil in a skillet. (Do not burn). Add flour and stir in, continuing cooking only about a minute. Add a cup of the broth and stir until flour is dissolved, smoothly.

Transfer skillet ingredients to a soup kettle. Add all other ingredients (except the parsley, salt and pepper) and bring to a boil. Reduce heat to simmer and cook (bubbly) for 40 minutes, stirring occasionally.

Add salt and pepper to taste.

Remove bay leaves before serving.

Pour into bowls and garnish with parsley.

Japanese Chicken Broth

Ingredients to serve 4:

4 cups water
2 chicken bouillon cubes
1 T soy sauce
thinly sliced mushrooms or chopped chives for garnish

Place water, bouillon and soy sauce in a soup pot and bring to a boil. Reduce heat to simmer; cook 5 minutes.

Garnish bowls of soup with sliced mushrooms or chopped chives.

Mexican Tortilla Soup

Ingredients to serve 6:

2 cns. (14 oz.) chicken broth
1 cup water
1 large onion, chopped
1 4 oz. cn. chopped green chilies
1 T cumin seed
1 cn. whole kernel corn, drained (or fresh corn from 3 ears)
4 tomatoes, diced
4 cloves garlic, minced
1/8 pound butter or margarine (1/2 stick) or 4 T oil
1-1/2 cups cooked chicken, diced

6 oz. Monterey Jack cheese, shredded for garnish
2-1/2 cups tortilla chips, crushed, but not fine

Sauté the cumin, onions and garlic in the butter until onion is translucent. Transfer to soup pot. Add all ingredients except chips and cheese. Bring to a boil. Reduce heat and simmer 20 minutes.

Place the crushed chips in the bottom of each bowl. Ladle in the soup and garnish with the shredded cheese.

Polish Duck Soup (Czarnina)*

Cut up in pieces 1 duck and boil with 1 onion, 2 carrots, 4 ribs of celery, allspice, a bay leaf, 1 t marjoram for 1 hour. Then add 1 cup raisins, 30 prunes, 1 apple cut up in pieces. When fruits and meat and vegetables are done, mix 1/2 cup duck blood with 2 T flour and 2 T vinegar. Add to the soup and let cook slowly 1/2 hour. The blood should be diluted with vinegar to keep it form setting. Serve with potato dumplings boiled separately.

Potato Dumplings:

Grate 4 or 5 large potatoes, pour off the accumulated water and add 1/2 cup flour, a pinch of baking powder, and a T salt and boil in salted water. (Drop 1/2 t dough at a time into the boiling water to form dumplings.) Drain in cold water and serve separately. Don't add them to the boiling soup, just in your soup dish.

Polish Fish Soup (Zupa z Ryby)*

Use as many different kinds of fresh fish as are available. Wash and clean fish (use all those too small for other use). Place fish in large kettle. Cover with water, salt and pepper to taste. Add 1 onion, 2 bay leaves, about 6 peppercorns or whole allspice. Celery and carrots also can be used for flavor. Bring to a boil. Add 1/2 cup of cold water, do this 3 times as it keeps the fish firm. Then cook slowly for an hour or so. Either drain or carefully remove fish from broth. To about 1/2 cup of sour cream add a small amount of the hot broth into the sour cream slowly. When broth and cream are blended put back on fire to heat. Add more pepper for flavor. To serve pour soup over boiled potato, or serve a bowl of potatoes if desired.

NOTE: We have used large fish heads, fins and back bones from fresh fish. Then just drain the broth to use as soup. This is a very good old Polish recipe for people who live near a lake and have fresh fish available.

*Courtesy Kay Bargen, Deerwood, MN

Portuguese Clam Soup

Ingredients to serve 4:

1 small cn. consommé soup
1 small cn. (about 8 oz.) minced clams
2 cups fresh peas or 1 cn. small peas
2 T butter or margarine
salt and pepper to taste
dill sprig for garnish (or parsley flakes)

Place all ingredients, including the juice from the canned clams, in a
soup pot. Bring to a boil; reduce heat to simmer. Cook 30 minutes.
Bring heat up and serve as soon as it starts to boil.
Garnish with dill or parsley.

Russian Borsch

Ingredients to serve 6:

8 cups water
1 pound lean beef, cut into 1 inch chunks
1 T salt
1 large onion, broken into rings
10 peppercorns
3 medium size beets, sliced
1 rib celery, chopped
1 large carrot, sliced
2 cups shredded cabbage
1 tomato, diced
2 bay leaves
2 T vegetable oil
1 T flour

Bring water to boiling in a large kettle. Add 1 T salt, peppercorns and
stew meat. Reduce heat and let simmer 30 minutes.

In a sauce pan, cover the beet slices with water. Cook over medium
heat until tender.

Add beets and all other ingredients to the meat pot. Cook another 30
minutes or until the meat is tender. Serve hot.

In some areas, it is a tradition to add a little sour cream to each bowl
as it is served.

The thickness of the soup varies with personal taste - all the way from
more of a broth to the thickness of stew.

Russian Fish Soup

Ingredients to serve 6:

2 pounds fish, scaled and cleaned
1/2 pound potatoes, cut into bite-sized chunks
2 medium carrots, sliced
5 tomatoes, blanched and peeled, quartered
1 large onion, sliced
2 T lemon juice
8 peppercorns
2 quarts of water
salt to taste
dill or parsley for garnish

Cut the cleaned and scaled fish into 2 or 3 inch chunks (original recipes used the heads - there is a lot of good meat in the cheeks). Place all ingredients except the fish in a kettle of cold water. Bring to a gentle boil and cook for about 10 minutes. Add the fish and continue cooking until the fish flakes easily and the vegetables are done. Skim off anything that comes to the surface.
Garnish with dill or parsley.

Spanish Garlic Soup

Ingredients to serve 8:

8 cups chicken broth
3 T garlic, minced
4 cups bread crumbs (traditionally dark bread and coarse crumbs)
1 - 16 oz. cn. tomatoes, diced
salt and freshly ground pepper to taste
2/3 cup cooking oil (traditional olive oil)
parsley for garnish

Sauté the garlic a couple of minutes; stir in the bread crumbs and cook over moderate heat until both the garlic and the bread crumbs are golden. The crumbs should be a little on the crisp side. Add remaining ingredients. Bring to a boil and then reduce to simmer. Let simmer at least 20 minutes.
Garnish servings with parsley.

Swedish Crayfish Soup

Ingredients to serve 6:

2 dozen freshwater crayfish (live)
6 cups water (modern recipes call for beef bouillon)
1/2 pound potatoes, quartered
2 large onions, chopped
3 medium carrots, sliced
2 cups white wine
1 bay leaf
1 cup cream
8 peppercorns (white, if available)
1 t marjoram
3 T butter
3 T flour

Sauté the onion in the butter. To 6 cups of water or bouillon, add the spices and the vegetables. Bring to a boil and add the crayfish. Boil for 15 minutes. While the soup cooks for another 10 minutes, remove and shell the crayfish tails. Cut tails into 2 or 3 pieces. Skim the soup, add the cream and the crayfish tails. Add the flour to the butter you used to sauté the onion. Stir into the soup.

Remove bay leaf before serving.

Check for flavor and add seasonings if necessary. Serve hot.

Welsh Potato Soup

Ingredients to serve 6:

4 medium potatoes, peeled and cut into 1/2 inch cubes
1 large onion, chopped coarse
1 cup green onions, (leeks) chopped (use white portion only but save greens)
3 T celery, chopped
1 cup milk
2 T vegetable oil
salt and pepper to taste
5 cups water to boil potatoes

Boil the potatoes in salted water until soft.

Sauté the celery, onion and white portion of green onions in oil until onion is translucent. Purée the potatoes and water (in small batches) in a blender.

Place all contents back in the soup kettle and simmer for 5 minutes, stirring. Stir in milk. Increase heat; continue to stir. Remove from heat as it starts to boil.

Garnish with finely chopped onion greens.

Part III
CHILLED SOUPS

Avocado with Lime

Ingredients to serve 6:

3 avocados, pitted and peeled, cut into chunks
1 lime, juice only
2 cups chilled water
1-1/2 cups half and half
1-1/2 cups chicken broth (or stock)
1 t chili powder (level or rounded according to taste)
1 t powdered cumin
salt and pepper to taste

In a blender, place the chunks of avocado, lime juice, broth, half and half, chilled water, cumin, chili powder and salt and pepper. Blend in batches if necessary. Transfer to a bowl. Cover and chill 2 hours (longer than 3 hours may discolor the soup). If not cold enough, place in freezer compartment of refrigerator last 15 minutes.
Soup may be garnished with a glob of sour cream.

Celery with Beets

Ingredients to serve 5-6:

4 ribs celery, chopped thin
3 cups chicken broth or stock
6 medium beets, peeled and diced
2 T sugar
1 onion, minced
1/2 cup dry red wine
1 clove garlic, minced
3 t olive oil
salt and pepper to taste

Cook the celery, onion and garlic in the olive oil until tender.

Transfer to a soup pot. Add all other ingredients except the wine and cook over medium heat until beets are tender. Let cool. Add wine.

Using a blender, purée in batches until smooth. Thin with ice water if consistency is too thick. Add salt and pepper if needed.

Chill several hours until very cold.

Peach with Yogurt

Ingredients to serve 5-6:

8 peaches, peeled, pitted, diced and quick-frozen
2 cups orange juice, chilled
3 T sugar
4 cups yogurt (blueberry, if available)
2 cups frozen blueberries

Stir the sugar into the diced peaches.

In a blender, purée the peaches and orange juice. Do it in two batches, using half of each of the ingredients each time.

Combine with the yogurt.

Meanwhile, rinse the frozen berries (in a colander), just for a minute or two.

Serve the soup in bowls with the berries sprinkled on top.

Apple Soup

Ingredients to serve 8:

6 hard apples, cored and chopped
6 cups water
2 cinnamon sticks (about 8 inches in all)
1 T lemon juice
6 T sugar
4 pieces cinnamon toast, crumbled
1 cup heavy cream

Place water, apples, cinnamon sticks, lemon juice and sugar in a soup kettle.

Bring to a boil, reduce heat to simmer and cook 30 minutes or until apple pieces are soft. Let cool.

Discard cinnamon sticks.

In a blender, purée soup in batches. Strain through a sieve.

Refrigerate 4 hours or more (covered).

Serve in bowls over crumbled cinnamon toast. Pour a little cream on top. (cream may be whipped).

Asparagus with Onion

Ingredients to serve 6:

2 pkgs. frozen asparagus, thawed and chopped (may substitute fresh)
2 large, sweet onions
1/4 pound butter or margarine (1 stick) or 8 T oil
1 large potato peeled and chopped
6 cups chicken broth or stock
1/2 cup dry white wine
1 T thyme
1 cup yogurt
1/2 t marjoram
1/2 t nutmeg
1 T parsley flakes
salt and pepper to taste
chopped chives for garnish

Sauté onions and asparagus in the butter for 4–5 minutes, stirring constantly so that onions do not burn. Transfer to a soup pot. Add all other ingredients except wine and yogurt. Salt and pepper to taste.

Bring to a boil; reduce heat to simmer. Cook 30 minutes or until potato is tender. Remove from heat and let cool. Stir in wine. Add salt or pepper if necessary.

Using a slotted spoon, set aside 2 cups of solids. Purée the balance in batches until smooth. Combine solids with puréed soup. If too thick, add ice water.

Refrigerate at least 5 hours.

Stir in yogurt just before serving. Garnish with chives.

Cucumber Soup

Ingredients to serve 4-5:

3 medium cucumbers, peeled and sliced very thin
1 sweet onion, sliced and broken into rings
3 T salt

2 garlic cloves, minced
2 t parsley flakes
3 cups half and half
1 cup plain yogurt
7 drops Tabasco sauce (or to taste)

Place the cucumber slices in a flat bowl or glass baking dish. Sprinkle with salt. Let sit 30 minutes. Rinse and drain.

Transfer cucumber slices to a bowl. Add all other ingredients. Stir together, thoroughly.

Chill at least 4 hours.

Tomato Soup

Ingredients to serve 6-8:

12 medium tomatoes, diced
1 onion, chopped
3 cloves garlic, minced
1 sm. cn. Jalapeno peppers (4 oz.) chopped
4 cups chicken broth
2 T lemon juice
salt and pepper to taste
2 avocados for garnish (optional)

Combine all ingredients in a soup pot. Bring to a boil, then reduce heat to simmer. Cook 20 minutes. Cool.

Purée in batches in a blender. Force through a sieve.

Salt and pepper to taste.

Chill about 4 hours.

Optional: For avocado garnish, purée the meat of 2 avocados with 3 T lemon juice. Float a large spoonful on top of each bowl served.

Rhubarb Soup

Ingredients to serve 6-8:

10 cups chopped rhubarb
8 cups water
2 sticks cinnamon (about 6"-8" total)
3 cups sugar
ice cream

Place all ingredients in a stainless steel or ceramic kettle. Bring to a boil, then reduce heat to simmer and cook 1 hour or until rhubarb is very soft and tender.

Discard cinnamon sticks. Let cool.

Set aside 2 cups.

Purée the balance in a blender in batches.

Combine the solids and the purée. Refrigerate 4 hours.

To serve, start with a scoop of vanilla or cinnamon ice cream in each bowl. Pour the soup over the ice cream.

Fruit Soup

Ingredients to serve 6:

2 cups chopped rhubarb
1 cup sugar
1 cup water
1 T grated ginger root
1 cantaloupe, peeled, seeded and diced
1 honey-dew melon, peeled, seeded and diced
1 cup orange juice
1 cup fruit (any) flavored yogurt lightly sprinkled with pepper

Place the rhubarb, sugar and water in a stainless steel or ceramic kettle. Bring to a boil, then reduce heat to simmer. Cook 1 hour or until rhubarb is very tender. Let cool.

Set aside half the rhubarb, melon meat and orange juice.

Stir together the remaining ingredients, add a dash or two of pepper and purée in small batches in a blender.

Combine the purée with the set-aside ingredients. Chill, covered, at least 4 hours.

Scandinavian Fruit Soup

Ingredients to serve 8:

2 quarts water
1/2 cup raisins
1 cup prunes, sliced
1 cup apricots, sliced (or peaches or other fruit)
juice of 1/2 orange
juice of 1/2 lemon

1/2 cup sugar
1/2 cup tapioca
1/2 t salt
1 stick cinnamon

Place the fruit in the water; bring to a boil and then reduce heat and let simmer about 20 minutes. Let cool. Add all other ingredients and cook until the tapioca is transparent. Serve cold.

Cantaloupe Soup

Ingredients to serve 6:

6 cups diced cantaloupe
1 cn. peach nectar (comes frozen; let thaw)
1 T ginger, grated
1 cup yogurt
3 T sugar

Combine all of the ingredients, thoroughly. Purée in batches until smooth.
Refrigerate for at least 2 hours. Also chill soup bowls.
Garnish with a sprig of parsley.

Part III
STEWS

Old Fashioned Irish Stew

Ingredients to serve 6:

2 pounds lean lamb or veal, cubed (about 3/4 inch). You may add a couple of sprigs of dill to the stew while cooking
3 T vegetable oil
2 onions, separated into rings
3 carrots, chunked (thick slices)
1 parsnip or turnip if available, sliced
6 cups beef broth
8 medium potatoes, quartered
2 T celery, chopped
salt and pepper to taste
chives or parsley for garnish, chopped

Brown the veal along with the onions and celery in the oil in the cooking pot. Add all other ingredients (with a dash of salt and pepper) except garnish. Bring to a boil then reduce heat to simmer. Let cook about 2 hours or until meat and vegetables are tender. You may have to add water from time to time.
Add salt and pepper to taste before serving. Garnish with chopped chives or parsley.

Camp Stew

Ingredients to serve 6-8:

2 pounds chuck or pot roast, cut into 1 inch cubes (bite-size)
1/2 cup flour
1 large onion, chopped (coarse)
1 pound small, whole sweet onions, peeled
4 T cooking oil

1 large can tomato soup (24 oz.)
1 can V-8 juice (12 oz.)
1 T salt
6 whole black peppers
8 medium carrots (sliced)
1 pkg. frozen peas
2 pounds small or cut potatoes
4 cups water

Roll the meat pieces in flour. Brown the meat and chopped onion in cooking oil over low heat. Add water and bring to a boil. Add tomato soup, V-8 juice, salt and peppers; let simmer for 2 hours. Add small onions, carrots, potatoes and peas and cook covered for about 30 minutes or until the vegetables are done. For spicier stew, add 1/2 cup catsup.

Depression Stew*

During the Great Depression of the 1930's this recipe was developed on the Iron Range of Minnesota. Wieners were very cheap in those days and were used as a "steak extender". Nowadays, the steak "extends the wieners"!

Ingredients to serve 4:

1 lb. round steak (beef, venison or other wild game) cut lean meat into 1 inch squares
1 lb. wieners-cut into 1/2 inch slices
1 cup catsup
1 cup water
1 large sliced onion
salt and pepper
1/2 cup celery, chopped
1/4 cup green pepper, chopped
1/2 cup brown sugar

Place the steak pieces in a large cast iron frying pan. Cover with water. Add a dash each of salt and pepper. Bring to a boil; reduce heat to simmer and cook for 1 hour.
Add all other ingredients and simmer for another hour or so until steak is tender.
Serve over boiled potatoes.

*Courtesy Mike Matanich, Staples, MN

Fish Stew

Ingredients to serve 4:

1 pound fillets, skinned and cut into 2 inch chunks
3 tomatoes, cut into 1/2 inch chunks
2 cloves garlic, minced
1 medium zucchini, slice thin (1/4")
1/2 cup chopped celery
1 onion, chopped coarse
1 cup potatoes pre-cooked (but still fairly hard) and sliced
3 carrots, pre-cooked (but still fairly hard) and sliced
1 bay leaf
oil, butter or margarine
1 cup white wine
3 cups water
salt and white pepper to taste
1/2 cup parsley flakes (for garnish) or 2 T chopped chives

Sauté the onion, celery, garlic and zucchini until the onion is translucent.

Add the water, wine and tomato pieces and bring to a boil. Reduce heat and let simmer 5 minutes. Add all other ingredients (except parsley) and bring to a boil. Reduce heat and let simmer another 5 minutes or until the fish flakes easily.

Remove bay leaf before serving.

Serve in bowls; garnish with parsley flakes or chopped chives.

Small Game Mulligan

Ingredients to serve 8:

Use whatever small game is available—squirrel, rabbit, partridge, pheasant, duck, etc. Don't hesitate to mix the game; the greater the variety the better. This recipe calls for about 1-1/2 pounds deboned meat.

Cut meat from the bone. Cut into bite-size chunks. Dredge in seasoned flour and brown in oil.

Cover with water, season with salt and pepper, and simmer 1 to 2 hours.

Then add the following:

1 #2 can tomatoes
1/2 cup wild rice, uncooked
1/2 cup catsup or 2 cns. tomato soup (or some of each)
1 large onion, sliced
2 beef bouillon cubes (if no poultry meat is used, use 4 cubes and no chicken bouillon)
2 chicken bouillon cubes (if no red meat is used, use 4 cubes and no beef bouillon)
2 large carrots, sliced
1 turnip, sliced
3 large potatoes, peeled and diced
1/2 cup celery, chopped
2 T parsley, chopped

Let simmer 3 hours. Pour off liquid or add water for desired "thickness".

Big Game Stew

Ingredients to serve 6-8:

2 pounds roast meat. Bake until tender, then cut into bite-size chunks. (Left-over roast works well).
Prepare 1/2 cup wild rice by covering with 3 cups water and simmering 1-1/2 hours or until rice flowers.
In a large kettle, place:

2 cns. vegetable beef stew
1 #2 cn. tomatoes
1 cn. mixed vegetables
2 small cns. cream of tomato soup
the cooked wild rice
2 T catsup

Add the meat chunks and heat (about 30 minutes on a medium burner).

Traditional Beef Stew

Ingredients to serve 4-6:

2 pounds beef roast (may use cheaper cuts)
4 tomatoes, blanched and peeled
4 potatoes, cubed
3 carrots, thick sliced
1 stalk celery, chopped
2 onions, sliced

2 T flour
8 allspice (whole)
8 peppercorns
1 laurel leaf
3 T cooking oil or fat
salt and pepper to taste
flour for browning

Cut the beef into bite-sized chunks. Roll in flour and brown in the oil after seasoning lightly with salt and pepper. Add the sliced onions during the last couple of minutes. Place meat and all other ingredients in a kettle (preferably iron) and stir in the flour and seasonings. Cover with water. Bring to a boil and then cut back the heat and let simmer until meat is tender.

A modern touch calls for the addition of 1/2 cup of catsup for a more "tomatoey" flavor. A can of tomato soup will produce similar results.

Chicken Stew

A generation or more ago, old or non-productive laying hens were butchered for stew. Today stewing hens are hard to come by, but the young, spring chickens available in today's markets work even better. Ingredients to serve 8:

2 chickens, skinned, de-boned and cut into bite-size chunks
1/4 pound butter or margarine (1 stick) or 8 T oil
1/2 cup flour
3 garlic cloves, minced
1 large onion, peeled, sliced and broken into rings
2 cups fresh mushrooms, sliced
2 zucchini squash, peeled and sliced thin
1 medium green pepper, seeded and chopped
2 potatoes, peeled and diced
2 cns. Italian style tomatoes
1 t poultry seasoning
1 t oregano
1 t basil
1 t thyme
1 t pepper
1/2 t salt

Roll the chicken pieces in the flour and sauté in butter until brown on all sides.

Remove chicken from skillet. Add more butter (or oil) if necessary and sauté onion, garlic, green pepper, mushrooms and zucchini about 3 minutes. Stir and shake; do not let burn.

Place all ingredients in a crock pot. Cook on high for 2 hours and on low for another 2 hours.

Serve as is or over boiled potatoes or biscuits.

Lamb Stew

Ingredients to serve 6-8:

2 pounds lamb, deboned and cut bite-size
1/2 cup flour
1/2 cup olive oil
2 zucchini squash, peeled and sliced thin
6 medium tomatoes, diced
4 garlic cloves, minced
1 green pepper, seeded and chopped
1 red (sweet) pepper, seeded and chopped
1 egg plant, cut bite-size
3 carrots, peeled and sliced
2 large onions, peeled, sliced and broken into rings
6 cups chicken broth
1 t cumin seeds
1/2 t ginger (powdered)
1/4 t ground allspice
2 cinnamon sticks (6-8 inches)
1 bay leaf
salt and pepper

Season the pieces of lamb with salt and pepper, dredge in flour and brown in the olive oil. Place lamb in a soup kettle. Cover lamb with water; bring to a boil, reduce heat and simmer for 1 hour.

Meanwhile, sauté the onion, peppers, zucchini, carrots, garlic and egg plant in the same pan and oil used to brown the meat. Stir and toss - about 5 minutes; do not let burn.

Place all ingredients - except the tomatoes - in the soup pot. Bring to a boil; reduce heat to simmer and cook for 1 hour or until lamb and vegetables are tender. Add tomatoes the last 10 minutes.

Remove bay leaf before serving.

Pork and Beef Stew

Ingredients to serve 6:

1 pound boneless lean beef, cubed (bite-size)
1 pound boneless lean pork, cubed (bite-size)
6 strips bacon
1 onion (medium) sliced and broken into rings
4 potatoes (medium) diced
2 carrots, scraped and sliced
1 cup sliced mushrooms of your choosing
1 cup white wine
1 cn. stewed tomatoes
1 t oregano
1/2 t black pepper
1/2 t salt
1 T paprika
water

Cut bacon into narrow strips (about 1/4 inch wide) and fry until "almost" crisp. Remove bacon from pan with a slotted spoon, but leave grease in pan.

Sauté the onions, mushroom slices and carrot slices in the bacon grease until onion is translucent. Remove ingredients from grease and discard grease.

Cover the diced beef and pork with water, add salt and pepper and bring to a boil - then reduce heat to simmer for about 1 hour or until meat is tender.

Add all remaining ingredients except wine and add more water until desired stew consistency is reached. Bring to a boil again, then reduce heat to simmer until all vegetables are tender.

Add wine and continue to heat for a few minutes so that stew is piping hot.

To thin stew, add water; to thicken stew, stir in a T or 2 of all purpose flour.

Cowboy Stew

Ingredients to serve 8:

2 pounds beef, cut bite-size
1/2 cup flour
3 T cooking oil
3 t beef bouillon granules
2 cups water
4 carrots, peeled and sliced thick
2 potatoes, peeled and cut bite-size
1 cn. tomatoes
1 cn. green beans, cut
1 large onion, peeled, sliced and broken into rings
3 cloves garlic, minced
1 cup salsa, medium
3 T catsup
1 T cumin seeds
1/4 t salt
1/2 t pepper
1 bay leaf

In a heavy skillet, brown the beef pieces in oil - after rolling them in flour.

Remove meat. Using the same skillet and oil (add more if necessary) sauté the onion and garlic until the onion pieces are clear.

In a soup pot, combine all ingredients. Bring to a boil, then reduce heat to simmer and cook until carrots, potatoes and beef are tender. (about 90 minutes). Remove bay leaf.

Serve over biscuits.

Veal Stew

Ingredients to serve 4-6:

2 pounds veal roast (may use cheaper cuts, such as neck or brisket)
4 potatoes, medium, cubed
3 carrots, medium, thick slices
1 large onion, sliced
1/2 cup celery, chopped

6 peppercorns
2 stalks dill, or 2 T dill seed
salt (1 T for parboiling and 1 t while making stew)

Cut the veal into bite-size chunks (about 1 inch cubes). Cover with water, add a little salt (1 T) and boil for about 20 minutes. Pour off water and rinse meat. Return meat to kettle and add all vegetables and seasonings except the potatoes. Cover with water. When the meat chunks are quite tender, add the cubed potatoes. If at any point the stew seems too thick, add water.

Oyster Stew

Ingredients to serve 4:

1 pt. oysters
1 qt. half and half
1/8 t curry powder
4 T butter or margarine
salt and pepper to taste

Combine all ingredients in a soup pot. Cook piping hot but do not let boil.
Serve with crackers and cold butter.

Oyster Stew with a Touch of Mushrooms

Ingredients to serve 6:

2 cups oysters, drained
3 T butter or margarine, melted
1 T minced onion
3 T mushrooms, chopped
1 qt. half and half
salt and pepper to taste

Sauté the oysters in the butter along with the onion and mushrooms. When the onion is translucent (2 or 3 minutes at most) add the milk. Heat thoroughly but do not let boil.
Season to taste. Serve with crackers and cold butter.

Part V
CHILI RECIPES

Vegetarian Chili

Ingredients to serve 8:

3 T cooking oil
1 large onion, peeled and chopped
3 ribs celery, chopped
1 green (bell, sweet) pepper, seeded and chopped
3 cloves garlic, minced
3 cns. hot kidney beans
1 cn. whole kernel corn, drained
2 cns. Mexican or Italian tomatoes
1 sm. cn. tomato soup
1/2 cup raisins
1/2 cup cashew nuts
1/4 cup red wine
3 t chili powder
1 T cumin, ground
1 T oregano
Tabasco, add a few drops if chili is not hot enough
shredded cheese for garnish

Sauté the onions, celery, pepper and garlic in the cooking oil (until onions are clear, about 3 minutes.)
Combine all ingredients except the nuts and wine in a large soup pot. Bring to a boil, then reduce heat to simmer and cook 1 hour.
Add wine and increase heat until chili is barely bubbly and cook another 10 minutes.
Add cashews as you serve.
Garnish with shredded cheese.

Chili Southwest Style

Ingredients to serve 6:

2 T cooking oil
2 pounds round steak, cut bite-size
3 cns. kidney beans
1 large onion, peeled and chopped
2 ribs celery, chopped
1 4 oz. cn. jalapeno peppers
1 cup salsa (mild, medium or hot - your choice)
2 cloves garlic, minced
1 t cumin, ground
1 t chili powder
shredded cheese of your choice for topping

Place the cubed steak in a saucepan and cover with water. Bring to a boil and then reduce heat. Let simmer 1 hour or until meat is tender. Meanwhile, sauté the onion, celery and garlic in the cooking oil. (about 3 minutes or until the onion is translucent).
Combine all ingredients (including water used to cook steak) in a large soup pot. Bring to a boil, then reduce heat so chili is just bubbly. Cook 1 hour. Serve with shredded cheese on top of each bowl.

Crock Pot Chili

Ingredients to serve 8:

2 pounds hamburger
3 cns. kidney beans
2 cns. Mexican (or Italian) style tomatoes
1 large onion, peeled and chopped
3 ribs celery, chopped
3 garlic cloves, minced
1 cn. tomato soup
1 sm. cn. (4 oz.) jalapeno peppers, chopped (use kitchen gloves)
1 T cumin, powdered
1 T chili powder
3 T cooking oil

Brown the hamburger, onion, celery and garlic together in a heavy skillet.
Combine all ingredients in the crock pot. Cook on high 1 hour and on low 2 hours. Actually, it can cook on low all day.

Ma's Chili*

Ingredients to serve 6:

1-1/2 pounds lean ground beef
2 cns. red kidney beans
3 cns. tomato soup
2 bell peppers, chopped
2 large onions, peeled and chopped
5 ribs celery, chopped
1 T chili powder
1 to 1-1/2 hot peppers, chopped (use kitchen gloves)
salt to taste

Make one day before serving; re-heat.
Brown the hamburger in a little oil. Cook the onions, celery and peppers at the same time.
Add all other ingredients. Bring to a boil, then reduce heat to simmer. Cook about 15 minutes.

*Courtesy Harol Wolfe, St. Cloud, MN

Chili Mountains*

In this recipe, the chili is prepared separately. Each guest ladles the chili over a "mountain" of cooked rice in a bowl covered with Frito chips. Garnishes of the guests' choosing are then added.

Ingredients to serve 10:

4 T cooking oil
2 pounds ground beef
2 onions, peeled and chopped
1 cup of chopped green pepper
1 large cn. tomatoes
1 large cn. tomato sauce
2 t chili powder
1 t salt
1/8 t cayenne pepper
1/8 t pepper
1 T cumin
1 clove garlic, minced
1 cn. kidney beans

Brown the ground beef, onions and garlic in the oil.
Place all ingredients in a soup pot, bring to a boil and then reduce heat

to simmer for 30 minutes.

Meanwhile, cook 3 cups of rice according to the directions on the box.

When the chili and the rice are done, let the guests serve themselves. On a counter, line up the food in this order: first the serving bowl of rice, next a bowl of Fritos or other chips, then the kettle of chili and last, small containers of the following garnishes:

fresh tomatoes, diced
onion, chopped
black olives, chopped
cheese, grated
green pepper, diced
sour cream
tomato sauce
Nacho cheese soup
jalapenos, chopped (handle with kitchen gloves when chopping)

*Courtesy Karen Schindler, Phoenix, AZ

Turkey/Chicken Chili

Ingredients to serve 4-6:

3 cups cooked turkey or chicken, cut bite-size
2 cns. hot kidney beans
2 cns. Mexican style tomatoes
1/8 pound butter or margarine (1/2 stick) or 4 T oil
1 onion, peeled and chopped
1 green pepper, peeled, seeded and chopped
1/2 cup sliced black olives
2 ribs celery, chopped
2 cloves garlic, minced
1/2 t oregano
1/2 t thyme
3 T butter
2 t chili powder
1 t cumin
6 T crumbled cheese of your choosing for topping (Monterey Jack works well)

Sauté the onion, celery and garlic in the butter (about 3 minutes or until the onion is translucent).

Place all ingredients (except the cheese) in a soup pot. Bring to a boil, then reduce heat to simmer for 20 minutes. Serve with crumbled or grated cheese on top of each bowl.

Quick Chili

Ingredients to serve 4:

1 pound hamburger
1 medium onion, chopped
2 ribs celery, chopped
3 T cooking oil
2 cns. hot kidney (chili) beans
1 cn. Italian or Mexican style tomatoes
1 cn. tomato soup
1 t cumin
1 T chili powder (or to taste)

In a heavy skillet or pot, brown the hamburger, celery and onion together (in the cooking oil).

Add all other ingredients. Bring to a boil; reduce heat to simmer (just so it is barely bubbly) and cook another 20 minutes.

Part VI
STOCKS

These stocks may be substituted for broth in soup recipes.

Chicken Stock

Ingredients:

2 quarts water
wings, neck, back and bones of 1 chicken
1 onion, peeled and sliced
4 cloves garlic, chopped
3 ribs celery, chopped
2 carrots, cut into chunks
10 peppercorns (black)
4 T chopped parsley
2 bay leaves

Place all ingredients in a soup kettle. Bring to a boil. Reduce to simmer for 3 hours. Skim froth regularly.
Let cool. Pour through a fairly fine sieve.
Stock may be kept, covered, under refrigeration a few days or may be frozen for future use.

Fish Stock

Ingredients:

2 quarts water
bones and trimmings (about 2 pounds) of white-meated fish
2 onions, peeled and sliced
4 T chopped parsley
1 rib celery, chopped
1/2 cup lemon juice
10 peppercorns (white)

Place all ingredients in a soup pot. Bring to a boil, then let simmer 30 minutes. Skim froth regularly. Let cool.

Strain through a sieve.

Keep covered in refrigerator (up to 3 days) or freeze.

Beef, Veal or Pork Stock

Ingredients:

5 pounds of bones (either beef, veal or pork) including about one pound of lean meat
4 ribs celery, chopped
3 onions, sliced
5 cloves garlic, chopped
4 carrots, scraped and sliced
1 large potato, peeled and diced
3 bay leaves
12 peppercorns
1 T thyme
5 qts. water

Place the bones in a roasting pan, with 2 cups of water. Roast in a preheated 350° oven, covered, 40 minutes. Add all vegetables and continue to roast another 40 minutes.

Transfer ingredients except the liquid to a large soup pot. Add the water and spices. Bring to a boil, then reduce heat to simmer for 6 hours.

Let cool. Skim off fat. Remove bones and strain out the vegetables and all other solids. Save only the liquid. Refrigerate at least 3 hours. Skim off any fat. Stock is now ready to use or may be frozen for future use.

ADDENDUM

Generic Base for Cream Soups

Ingredients to serve 10-12:

2 cups powdered milk
3 T onion flakes (dried)
2 t dried parsley flakes
3 T cornstarch
4 T powdered bouillon - chicken or beef
1 t basil
1 T poultry seasoning
1/2 t pepper
1/4 t salt

Mix all ingredients and store in an air-tight container.

When you are ready to make soup, be sure ingredients of base are well mixed, then use the proportion you need (one-half of mixture to make 5-6 cups, etc.)

Add 2 cups of water for half the mix or 4 cups for all of it. Stir thoroughly. The base is now ready for making any of the cream soup recipes - just add the main ingredient: onions or mushrooms or celery or whatever. Bring to a boil, then reduce to simmer and cook until main ingredient is done.

Personal Recipes

Personal Recipes

Personal Recipes

Personal Recipes

Other Books by Duane Lund

Andrew, Youngest Lumberjack
A Beginner's Guide to Hunting and Trapping
A Kid's Guidebook to Fishing Secrets
Early Native American Recipes and Remedies
Fishing and Hunting Stories from The Lake of the Woods
Lake of the Woods, Yesterday and Today, Vol. 1
Lake of the Woods, Earliest Accounts, Vol. 2
Our Historic Boundary Waters
Our Historic Upper Mississippi
Tales of Four Lakes and a River
The Youngest Voyageur
White Indian Boy
Nature's Bounty for Your Table
The North Shore of Lake Superior, Yesterday and Today
Leech Lake, Yesterday and Today
Gull Lake, Yesterday and Today
101 Favorite Freshwater Fish Recipes
101 Favorite Wild Rice Recipes
101 Favorite Mushroom Recipes
Camp Cooking, Made Easy and Fun
Sauces, Seasonings and Marinades for Fish and Wild Game
The Scandinavian Cookbook
101 Ways to Add to Your Income
The Indian Wars
Gourmet Freshwater Fish Recipes
Traditional Holiday Ethnic Recipes - collected all over the world
Entertainment Helpers, Quick and Easy

About the Author

- SENIOR CONSULTANT TO THE BLANDIN FOUNDATION
- EDUCATOR (RETIRED, SUPERINTENDENT OF SCHOOLS, STAPLES, MINNESOTA);
- HISTORIAN (PAST MEMBER OF EXECUTIVE BOARD, MINNESOTA HISTORICAL SOCIETY); Past Member of BWCA and National Wilderness Trails Advisory Committees;
- TACKLE MANUFACTURER (PRESIDENT, LUND TACKLE CO.);
- WILDLIFE ARTIST, OUTDOORSMAN.